STATISTICAL AND COMPARATIVE STUDIES
OF THE AUSTRALIAN ABORIGINAL DENTITION

STATISTICAL AND COMPARATIVE STUDIES OF THE AUSTRALIAN ABORIGINAL DENTITION

Kazuro HANIHARA
University of Tokyo

UNIVERSITY OF TOKYO PRESS

The University Museum, The University of Tokyo, Bulletin No. 11, 1976

© University of Tokyo Press, 1976
UTP 3045-68557-5149
Printed in Japan.
All rights reserved. No part of this publication may be reproduced or transmitted in any form or by any means, electronic or mechanical, including photocopy, recording, or any information storage and retrieval system, without permission in writing from the publisher.

ISBN 0-86008-171-0

TO THE LATE DR MURRAY J. BARRETT

CONTENTS

1. Introduction 1
2. Materials Used 2
3. Methods of Investigation... 4
   3.1. Measurements 4
   3.2. Observations 4
   3.3. Statistical Computations 4
4. Tooth Crown Measurements 6
   4.1. Comparison of Individual Teeth between Populations 6
      4.1.1. Deciduous Dentition 6
      4.1.2. Permanent Dentition 9
      4.1.3. Depth of Lingual Fossa in the Permanent Maxillary Central Incisors.. 15
   4.2. Sex Difference in Mesiodistal Crown Diameters as a Whole 18
   4.3. Comparison of Mesiodistal Crown Diameters between Yuendumu and Queensland Materials 21
   4.4. Principal Component Analysis.................................... 23
      4.4.1. Principal Component Analysis of the Mesiodistal Crown Diameters.. 23
      4.4.2. Comparison of Populations in Terms of Principal Components of the Mesiodistal Crown Diameters 30
   4.5. Distance Analysis 32
      4.5.1. Mahalanobis' Generalized Distance Based on the Mesiodistal Crown Diameters in the Permanent Dentition 32
      4.5.2. Penrose's Shape Distance Based on the Mesiodistal Crown Diameters of the Permanent and Deciduous Dentitions 35
5. Non-Metric Tooth Crown Characters 38
   5.1. Description of Non-Metric Crown Characters Used in the Present Study.. 38
   5.2. Frequencies of Non-Metric Crown Characters in the Permanent Dentition 40
   5.3. Frequencies of Non-Metric Crown Characters in the Deciduous Dentition 42
   5.4. Affinities of Populations Viewed from Biological Distance Based on the Non-Metric Crown Characters 43
6. Discussion 49

7. Summary and Conclusions 51
Acknowledgements 54
References.. 55

1. INTRODUCTION

Since Campbell (1925) reported dental characteristics in the Australian Aborigines, a considerable number of investigations on dentition of this population have been carried out. In particular, works of the project team of Department of Dental Science, the University of Adelaide, should be borne in mind. This project started in the early 1950's under the direction of M. J. Barrett to make longitudinal studies on dentition of Aborigines known as Wailbri who lived under settlement conditions at Yuendumu, 185 miles northwest of Alice Springs in Central Australia. Since then they have accumulated extensive data including excellent dental casts, part of which is composed of deciduous and permanent dentitions in the same individuals.

Very fortunately, the present author had an opportunity to visit the University of Adelaide to investigate the collection of dental casts in 1969. During a four-month stay in Adelaide, he made researches including dental crown measurements and observations, and took a number of photographs of dental crowns. Although several papers on dentition of Yuendumu Aborigines have been published so far by Barrett and his colleagues, the present author paid special attention to affinities of Aborigines to some other populations on which the data were obtained by himself.

Since the greater part of this investigation had to be aided by computer facilities, the final analyses started after the required computer programs had been developed. This is one of the reasons why the publication of this paper has been delayed.

There are still some other problems which should be discussed in regard to overall dental characteristics represented by Aborigines, and to origin as well as diversification of this population viewed from dental anthropology. However, the data obtained by the present study are not necessarily sufficient to solve such problems so that they remain for the future investigations.

2. MATERIALS USED

The materials used in this study were plaster casts of the permanent and deciduous dentitions in Aborigines and several other populations (Table 1).

The samples of Aborigines were selected from the dental casts obtained at the Yuendumu Settlement in Central Australia. These casts were made by the survey of

Table 1. Materials Used

Population	Dentition	Sex	No. of Materials	Collection of
Aborigine	Permanent	Male	95	Dept. of Dental Science The Univ. of Adelaide
		Female	67	As above
	Deciduous	Male	65	As above
		Female	58	As above
Japanese	Permanent	Male	50	Dept. of Anthropology The Univ. of Tokyo*
		Female	50	As above*
	Deciduous	Male	60	As above*
		Female	60	As above*
Ainu	Permanent	Male	20	As above*
		Female	14	As above*
	Deciduous	Male	12	As above*
		Female	10	As above*
Pima	Permanent	Male	60	Dept. of Anthropology The Univ. of Chicago
		Female	60	As above
	Deciduous	Male	63	As above
		Female	57	As above
Caucasian (in U.S.A.)	Permanent	Male	47	As above
		Female	35	As above
	Deciduous	Male	30	As above
		Female	32	As above
American Negro	Permanent	Male	40	Dept. of Orthodontics Howard University
		Female	40	As above
	Deciduous	Male	25	Dept. of Anthropology The Univ. of Chicago
		Female	29	As above
Alaska Eskimo	Permanent	Unknown	30	U.S. National Museum
	Deciduous	Unknown	21	As above

* Specimens are now stored in Dept. of Anthropology and Prehistory, The University Museum, The University of Tokyo.

Department of Dental Science, the University of Adelaide, and are now stored in the same Department.

The Japanese samples were obtained from children of kindergartens and high school pupils living in the Tokyo and Hokkaido areas. The Ainu samples were from inhabitants of Hidaka District, the southern part of Hokkaido, whose rate of admixture with the ordinary Japanese had been estimated to be less than 1/2. The materials of American Caucasians were obtained from those living in Chicago, and the American Negro materials were from those living in Washington, D.C., whose rate of admixture with Caucasians was unknown. The Pima Indian materials were selected from the extensive collection of Department of Anthropology, the University of Chicago. All of these materials were directly measured and observed by the present author.

In addition, the data provided by previous authors were also used in computation of some statistical analyses. However, in regard to non-metric characters of the dental crowns, only the data which had been obtained by direct observation of the present author were employed, because there might have been some discrepancies between investigators.

The present study covers all the dentition, both deciduous and permanent, with the exception of the permanent third molars. Most of the materials used in the present study consisted of plaster casts obtained from relatively young individuals for the purpose of making measurements and observations as precisely as possible. In this regard, the numbers of the third molars were so limited that reliable statistical treatment was hardly possible.

3. METHODS OF INVESTIGATION

3.1. Measurements

Measurements of dental crowns were made by ordinary sliding calipers calibrated to 0.1 mm, and mesiodistal crown diameters were obtained from the right side teeth, no buccolingual diameters having been measured because accurate measurements were hardly possible on plaster casts from the living. No measurements were made if the tooth was heavily worn or badly damaged, so that the sample numbers were different from tooth to tooth in almost every population investigated.

The measurements of the shovel-shaping of the incisors were made by a dial gauge with a pair of movable arms, and read to an accuracy of 0.05 mm (Hanihara et al., 1970).

3.2. Observations

Observations of the non-metric crown characters were made on the right side teeth, the left side teeth having been observed only when the antimeres were in bad condition. The criteria for classifying each character were generally based on the P-series plaques provided by Dahlberg for the permanent dentition, and the D-series plaques by Hanihara (1961) for the deciduous dentition. However, their detailed descriptions will be given in the relevant chapter.

3.3. Statistical Computations

Several statistical computations were processed by the HITAC-OS7 system of the University of Tokyo Computer Centre using FORTRAN programs coded by the

Table 2. FORTRAN Programs Used in the Present Study

Program Name	Purpose	Name of Package
BASIC1	Compute basic statistics from the raw data	PLAS*
INDEX2	Compute indices and related statistics	PLAS
PENROS	Compute Penrose's distance	PLAS
MAHADS	Compute generalized distances and canonical variates	PLAS
NONMET	Compute distances from frequencies of non-metric characters	PLAS
LFUNCT	Compute linear function using arbitrary coefficients	PLAS
CFACTR	Factor analysis	HSAP**
CPCOMP	Principal component analysis	HSAP
CQUAN4	Quantification model IV	HSAP

* Program Library for Anthropological Statistics, coded by K. Hanihara.
** Hitachi Statistical Analysis Program.

3. Methods of Investigation

present author and those contained in HSAP program package (Table 2). In addition, an electronic portable-type calculator was also used for calculation of relatively simple statistics.

4. TOOTH CROWN MEASUREMENTS

4.1. Comparison of Individual Teeth between Populations

4.1.1. Deciduous Dentition

In the first place, the mesiodistal crown diameters in the deciduous dentition were directly compared between Aborigines and other four populations studied by the present author.

It is quite obvious that all the deciduous teeth in Aborigines, both males and females, show the largest mesiodistal crown diameters among the five populations involved (Tables 3 and 4). However, the standard deviations in Aborigines are not significantly different from those of the remaining populations.

As to comparison between the present study and the data for the Aborigines which were reported by Campbell (1925) and Barrett et al. (1963), the former shows the largest values in the six deciduous teeth, and the latter provides the largest values in the remaining four deciduous teeth. Although the differences between each other are rather small, such discrepancies might have been caused by several reasons such as difference in areas from which the materials were obtained, difference in number of materials measured, slight difference in measuring technique between investigators, etc. However, even if the smallest values in Aborigines are taken into account, they still show the largest mean mesiodistal crown diameters among several populations including those studied by the present author and previous authors (Table 5). This finding evidently shows that Aborigines are one of the groups which carry the largest deciduous dentition among modern human populations.

To discuss the differences between Aborigines and the other populations in more detail, a t-test for significance of difference between means was carried out. In Table 6, minus signs show that the teeth in respective populations are significantly smaller than those of Aborigines at the 5% level.

As a whole, Aborigines exceed other populations in most of the mesiodistal crown diameters. There are, however, some teeth which show no significant difference from those of Aborigines. In particular, Pimas seem to carry the maxillary deciduous molars which are almost comparable with those of Aborigines in size. Almost the same trend, though to somewhat less extent, is also recognized in American Negroes in which four teeth show no significant difference from those of Aborigines.

On the other hand, Japanese and American Caucasians carry much smaller teeth than Aborigines, with the only exception of the maxillary first deciduous molar in Japanese.

In order to recognize the general trend of difference in each tooth, the ratio between mean values of Aborigines and grand means of other four populations were calculated. As can be seen in Table 7, differences in mesiodistal crown diameters are larger in the deciduous incisors and smaller in the deciduous molars. This trend is almost the same in either males or females, and in maxillary or mandiblular dentitions.

4. Tooth Crown Measurements

Table 3. Means and Standard Deviations of Mesiodistal Crown Diameters in the Male Deciduous Dentition

Tooth	Aborigine N	M	SD	Japanese N	M	SD	Pima N	M	SD	Caucasian N	M	SD	Am. Negro N	M	SD
di¹	32	7.31	.4413	60	6.70	.3843	51	6.86	.4348	10	6.40	.5034	3	6.03	.3215
di²	46	6.03	.2068	60	5.53	.3161	61	5.72	.3965	11	5.30	.4337	7	5.27	.3774
dc	63	7.35	.4806	60	6.70	.3266	61	7.15	.4376	27	6.80	.3409	23	6.86	.4143
dm¹	63	7.62	.5500	60	7.42	.3853	60	7.51	.4120	28	6.96	.3499	22	7.43	.4951
dm²	64	9.77	.3510	60	9.46	.4833	62	9.66	.4633	28	8.81	.5644	23	9.24	.4688
di₁	20	4.40	.3504	60	4.16	.3097	24	4.22	.3467	8	3.91	.4486	3	3.87	.3215
di₂	35	5.00	.3805	60	4.64	.3004	51	4.82	.2975	8	4.62	.4622	4	4.38	.3500
dc	60	6.18	.3731	60	5.88	.3081	63	6.20	.2889	23	5.81	.3935	22	6.05	.3635
dm₁	62	8.50	.5954	60	8.23	.3890	60	8.05	.3890	24	7.71	.4986	17	8.16	.5545
dm₂	63	11.10	.5588	60	10.36	.4227	62	10.62	.5073	25	9.70	.5478	19	10.21	.5217

Table 4. Means and Standard Deviations of Mesiodistal Crown Diameters in the Female Deciduous Dentition

Tooth	Aborigine N	M	SD	Japanese N	M	SD	Pima N	M	SD	Caucasian N	M	SD	Am. Negro N	M	SD
di¹	19	7.28	.3686	60	6.53	.4182	49	6.82	.4251	10	6.40	.3590	7	6.54	.4614
di²	36	6.03	.3700	60	5.42	.3350	53	5.62	.3329	12	5.35	.4189	15	5.33	.2498
dc	58	7.29	.4533	60	6.62	.3608	57	7.00	.3910	31	6.76	.3640	29	6.89	.3917
dm¹	57	7.38	.4325	60	7.27	.4179	55	7.31	.3613	30	6.83	.4367	28	7.32	.5014
dm²	57	9.59	.5596	60	9.29	.5306	56	9.46	.4747	31	8.68	.5010	28	9.19	.4459
di₁	11	4.60	.3745	60	4.07	.2826	14	4.09	.4048	8	3.95	.3162	4	4.10	.2450
di₂	22	5.00	.3363	60	4.56	.2902	44	4.80	.4088	11	4.62	.3629	8	4.69	.3604
dc	50	6.23	.3078	60	5.82	.3005	55	6.15	.3822	29	5.78	.4360	25	5.85	.3549
dm₁	55	8.28	.5664	60	8.10	.3790	53	7.98	.4401	31	7.64	.3834	27	8.10	.5262
dm₂	56	10.88	.5958	60	10.21	.4348	55	10.35	.5106	32	9.58	.5734	28	10.24	.4689

Table 5. Mean Mesiodistal Crown Diameters in the Deciduous Dentition Reported by Previous Authors

Sex	Tooth	Aborigine* (Campbell, '25)	Aborigine (Barrett et al., '63)	Swede (Seipel, '46)	Tristanite (Thomsen, '55)	Am. White (Moorrees et al., '57)
Male	di¹	7.8	7.40	6.60	6.57	6.55
	di²	6.0	6.19	5.46	5.26	5.32
	dc	7.5	7.52	7.04	6.41	6.88
	dm¹	8.0	7.73	7.31	7.13	7.12
	dm²	9.7	9.84	8.94	8.94	9.08
	di$_1$	4.7	4.52	4.25	4.03	4.08
	di$_2$	5.4	5.14	4.86	4.73	4.74
	dc̄	6.4	6.44	6.04	5.60	5.92
	dm$_1$	9.1	8.46	8.00	7.69	7.80
	dm$_2$	11.7	11.04	9.94	9.87	9.83
Female	di¹		7.29	6.56	6.41	6.44
	di²		6.14	5.36	5.34	5.23
	dc		7.31	6.93	6.47	6.67
	dm¹		7.49	7.18	6.88	6.95
	dm²		9.59	8.79	8.82	8.84
	di$_1$		4.52	4.16	4.03	3.98
	di$_2$		5.24	4.81	4.58	4.63
	dc̄		6.35	5.92	5.66	5.74
	dm$_1$		8.26	7.85	7.54	7.65
	dm$_2$		10.68	9.80	9.41	9.64

* Both sexes seem to be combined.

Barrett et al. (1963) stated that the most striking difference in tooth size between Aborigines and other groups had been shown by the mandibular deciduous second molars. However, if the same ratios as above are calculated from the data given by them, the deciduous incisors show still the largest difference between Aborigines and other populations. The present author will return to this point later.

The difference between sexes in the Aborigines is not so large. In fact, the significant differences are shown only by the maxillary and mandibular deciduous molars, and this trend is almost the same in the other modern human populations. Sex difference in overall size of the teeth will be discussed later.

Barrett et al. (1963) discussed variability in mesiodistal crown diameters of each tooth. Based on the coefficients of variation (100× s.d./mean), they found that the variability was greater in male subjects than in females with a minor exception. However, if the same coefficients are calculated from the data obtained by the present author, there seem to be no general trend in sex difference of the variability (Table 8).

For instance, five teeth show greater variability in females than in males of Aborigines, six teeth of Japanese and Pimas, four teeth of Caucasians, and three teeth of American Negroes. In addition, the teeth which show greater variability in males than in females are randomly distributed in the dentition. This seems to show that the difference in

Table 6. T-test for Difference in Mean Mesiodistal Crown Diameters between Aborigines and Other Populations

Sex	Tooth	Japanese	Pima	Caucasian	Am. Negro
Male	di^1	—	—	—	—
	di^2	—	—	—	—
	dc̲	—	—	—	—
	dm^1	—		—	
	dm^2	—		—	—
	di$_1$	—		—	—
	di$_2$	—	—	—	—
	dc̄	—		—	
	dm$_1$	—	—	—	—
	dm$_2$	—	—	—	—
Female	di^1	—	—	—	—
	di^2	—	—	—	—
	dc̲	—	—	—	—
	dm^1			—	
	dm^2	—		—	—
	di$_1$	—	—	—	—
	di$_2$	—	—	—	—
	dc̄	—	—	—	—
	dm$_1$	—		—	—
	dm$_2$	—	—	—	—

variability between sexes shows no general trend among modern human populations. On the other hand, difference in variability among the modern populations is also hardly detectable from the data shown in Table 8.

4.1.2. *Permanent Dentition*

In the present study, mesiodistal crown diameters in the permanent dentition of Aborigines were compared with those of Japanese, Pimas, Ainu, American Caucasians and American Negroes, all of which were measured by the present author (Tables 9 and 10).

As a whole, Aborigines exceed most of the other populations in crown size and this fact is comparable with the deciduous dentition. However, Aborigines are rather smaller than Pimas in some teeth. In males, nine teeth out of fourteen show larger mean values in Pimas than in Aborigines. The most striking difference is recognized in the maxillary canines, in which the mean mesiodistal crown diameter in Pimas amounts to 106.3% of that in Aborigines. Also in the mandibular canines, Pimas show 104.7% of Aborigines.

On the contrary, the maxillary lower molars of Aborigines are larger than those of Pimas. Almost the same trend is recognized when the tooth sizes for Pimas are compared with those of Aborigines reported by Campbell (1925) and Barrett et al. (1963)

Table 7. Comparison between Mean Mesiodistal Crown Diameters of Aborigines and Grand Mean of Four Populations (Deciduous Dentition)

Tooth	Aborigine (1)	Grand Mean (2)*	Ratio (1)/(2)%
di^1	7.31	6.50	112.46
di^2	6.03	5.46	110.44
$d\underline{c}$	7.35	6.88	106.83
dm^1	7.62	7.33	103.96
dm^2	9.77	9.29	105.17
di_1	4.40	4.04	108.91
di_2	5.00	4.62	108.23
$d\bar{c}$	6.18	5.99	103.17
dm_1	8.50	8.04	105.72
dm_2	11.10	10.22	108.61
di^1	7.28	6.57	110.81
di^2	6.03	5.43	111.05
$d\underline{c}$	7.29	6.82	106.89
dm^1	7.38	7.18	102.79
dm^2	9.59	9.16	104.69
di_1	4.60	4.05	113.58
di_2	5.00	4.67	107.07
$d\bar{c}$	6.23	5.90	105.59
dm_1	8.28	7.96	104.02
dm_2	10.88	10.10	107.72

* Grand Mean of Japanese, Pimas, Caucasians and Am. Negroes.

(Table 11). In Campbell's data, Aborigines are smaller than Pimas in six teeth out of fourteen, and ten teeth out of fourteen in the data provided by Barrett et al. At the same time, very similar difference can be seen in the data for females. These results likely suggest the predominance in size of particular teeth of Pimas over those of Aborigines.

As in the deciduous dentition, a t-test of difference of means between Aborigines and other populations was applied. In Table 12, minus signs show significantly smaller teeth and plus signs significantly larger teeth compared with those of Aborigines at the 5% level.

As described above, Japanese, Ainu and Caucasians show smaller values than Aborigines in most of the teeth. Pimas show larger values in the canines and some other front teeth, but almost the same or a little bit smaller values in the premolars and molars. On the other hand, American Negroes show smaller values than Aborigines in some teeth, but almost the same values in others.

It is quite interesting to note that overall size of the crowns in the deciduous dentition is the largest in Aborigines and followed by Pimas, but in the permanent dentition, Pimas exceed Aborigines in size of some teeth, and the latter is not necessarily the largest population in the tooth crown size among modern human populations.

4. Tooth Crown Measurements

Table 8. Coefficients of Variation (CV) in the Deciduous Dentition

Sex	Tooth	Aborigine	Japanese	Pima	Caucasian	Am. Negro
Male	di^1	6.04	5.74	6.34	7.87	5.33
	di^2	3.43	5.72	6.93	8.18	7.16
	$d\underline{c}$	6.54	4.87	6.12	5.01	6.04
	dm^1	7.22	5.19	5.49	5.03	6.66
	dm^2	3.59	5.11	4.80	6.41	5.07
	di_1	7.96	7.44	8.22	11.47	8.31
	di_2	7.61	6.47	6.17	10.00	7.99
	$d\bar{c}$	6.04	5.24	4.66	6.77	6.01
	dm_1	7.00	5.43	4.83	6.47	6.80
	dm_2	5.03	4.08	4.78	5.65	5.11
Female	di^1	5.06	6.40	6.23	5.61	7.06
	di^2	6.14	6.18	5.92	7.83	4.69
	$d\underline{c}$	6.22	5.45	5.59	5.38	5.69
	dm^1	5.86	5.75	4.94	6.31	6.85
	dm^2	5.84	5.71	5.02	5.77	4.85
	di_1	8.14	6.94	9.90	8.01	5.98
	di_2	6.73	6.36	8.52	7.85	7.68
	$d\bar{c}$	4.94	5.16	6.21	7.54	6.07
	dm_1	6.84	4.68	5.52	5.02	6.50
	dm_2	5.48	4.26	4.93	5.99	4.58

The mean values for Aborigines are always larger than those of populations reported by previous authors. The only exception may be seen in the lower molars between Aborigines reported by Barrett et al. (1963) and Aleut by Moorrees (1957). However, the mean value given by Barrett et al. seems to be too small compared with values given by Campbell (1925) and the present author.

In order to learn the general trend of the crown size in Aborigines, as in the deciduous dentition, ratios between mean mesiodistal crown diameters of Aborigines and grand means of those of Japanese, Pimas, Ainu, Caucasians and American Negroes were calculated (Table 13). In general, the ratios show small deviations from tooth to tooth, but relatively small in the canines and particularly large in the maxillary second molars, both males and females. This trend seems to show that the canines might be relatively stable in size, and on the contrary, the maxillary molars might be more variable among modern human populations. In other words, the maxillary molars in Aborigines seem to be less reduced in comparison with those of the other populations. On the other hand, the mandibular second molars show somewhat smaller ratios than the maxillary second molars, showing a little more stability of the former than the latter.

Sex difference in tooth crown size is relatively small in Aborigines. A student's t-test shows that a statistically significant difference exists only in the mandibular canines under the 1% level. This is quite comparable with most of the other populations compared.

On the other hand, Barrett et al. (1963) found significant sex differences in all the

Table 9. Means (romans) and Standard Deviations (italics) of Mesiodistal Crown Diameters in the Permanent Dentition (Male)

Tooth	Aborigine N	M & SD	Japanese N	M & SD	Pima N	M & SD	Ainu N	M & SD	Am. Caucasian N	M & SD	Am. Negro N	M & SD
I^1	77	9.25 *.5904*	50	8.65 *.4548*	60	9.14 *.3843*	20	8.38 *.4246*	47	8.63 *.6458*	39	9.06 *.5441*
I^2	77	7.53 *.5642*	50	7.13 *.5253*	60	7.68 *.3688*	20	7.18 *.3660*	46	6.63 *.5903*	40	7.13 *.6527*
$\underline{C}$	75	8.26 *.5258*	50	8.18 *.3615*	60	8.78 *.4812*	20	7.91 *.3227*	45	7.82 *.4485*	40	8.26 *.4411*
P^1	78	7.70 *.5082*	50	7.47 *.4268*	60	7.80 *.4588*	20	6.99 *.3838*	45	7.08 *.4350*	40	7.63 *.4580*
P^2	71	7.12 *.4601*	50	6.96 *.3430*	60	7.45 *.4470*	20	6.47 *.3275*	46	6.75 *.5053*	40	7.22 *.5194*
M^1	79	11.31 *.5167*	50	10.72 *.5087*	60	11.03 *.5406*	20	10.40 *.4537*	47	10.73 *.5969*	40	11.03 *.6022*
M^2	59	10.96 *.6153*	50	9.64 *.4896*	60	10.46 *.5292*	20	9.08 *.5566*	40	10.25 *.6037*	33	10.65 *.6419*
I_1	80	5.78 *.4144*	50	5.56 *.3632*	60	5.89 *.4281*	20	5.38 *.2607*	43	5.50 *.4254*	40	5.60 *.3258*
I_2	80	6.48 *.4125*	50	6.17 *.3473*	60	6.71 *.3935*	20	6.01 *.3355*	44	6.04 *.4746*	40	6.20 *.3860*
$\bar{C}$	77	7.42 *.4881*	50	7.10 *.3775*	60	7.77 *.3975*	20	7.09 *.3220*	45	6.93 *.4495*	39	7.31 *.5156*
P_1	78	7.53 *.5968*	50	7.30 *.3738*	60	7.61 *.4236*	20	6.95 *.3069*	44	7.10 *.3945*	40	7.77 *.4734*
P_2	71	7.63 *.5601*	50	7.19 *.3651*	60	7.67 *.5447*	20	6.69 *.3284*	41	7.30 *.5038*	40	7.75 *.5808*
M_1	78	11.99 *.8479*	50	11.49 *.4564*	60	11.80 *.4947*	20	11.23 *.5183*	45	11.24 *.6535*	39	12.01 *.6524*
M_2	59	11.55 *.6658*	50	10.56 *.6960*	60	11.47 *.5456*	20	10.45 *.7015*	34	10.83 *.7237*	27	11.47 *.7560*

teeth except for the third molars and the mandibular first premolars, and the most pronounced differences were found in the mandibular canines and the first molars. Although the same trend was recognized by the present author, there seem to be a minor discrepancy between the results of statistical tests carried out in the two investigations. It is rather doubtful, however, that Aborigines show much larger sex differences in comparison with the other populations, because the statistical significance does not necessarily represent the amount of difference which was tested. Further discussions on sex difference in tooth crown size will appear later.

Barrett et al. (1963) pointed out that, according to coefficients of variation, the third molars and the maxillary lateral incisors varied most in size and the first molars least. In the male samples of the present study, however, the mandibular first molar shows relatively large size variability (Table 14). The mesiodistal crown diameters of this tooth range from 10.50 mm to 13.60 mm which are almost comparable with those reported by Barrett et al. On the other hand, the female samples of the present study show very

4. Tooth Crown Measurements

Table 10. Means (romans) and Standard Deviations (italics) of Mesiodistal Crown Diameters in the Permanent Dentition (Female)

Tooth	Abrigine N	M & SD	Japanese N	M & SD	Pima N	M & SD	Ainu N	M & SD	Caucasian N	M & SD	Am. Negro N	M & SD
I^1	58	9.10 *.5848*	50	8.50 *.4561*	60	8.72 *.4276*	14	8.28 *.4354*	33	8.41 *.5237*	40	8.84 *.4065*
I^2	57	7.46 *.6730*	50	7.00 *.5299*	60	7.47 *.4528*	14	6.88 *.7797*	32	6.51 *.5598*	40	7.07 *.4967*
C	57	8.01 *.4947*	50	7.84 *.4578*	60	8.24 *.3351*	14	7.62 *.4475*	34	7.57 *.3452*	40	7.82 *.3969*
P^1	57	7.64 *.4205*	50	7.46 *.4131*	60	7.48 *.4034*	14	6.98 *.3534*	34	6.85 *.3979*	40	7.37 *.4666*
P^2	53	7.17 *.4657*	50	6.96 *.3988*	60	7.21 *.4176*	14	6.31 *.5097*	32	6.62 *.4589*	40	7.07 *.3986*
M^1	57	11.14 *.5911*	50	10.35 *.4400*	60	10.71 *.4831*	14	10.02 *.4406*	34	10.38 *.4532*	40	10.69 *.6211*
M^2	50	10.76 *.6967*	49	9.57 *.4367*	60	10.26 *.4759*	14	9.11 *.7026*	24	9.67 *.4428*	28	10.12 *.4757*
I_1	58	5.67 *.4012*	48	5.45 *.3054*	60	5.64 *.2964*	14	5.30 *.3531*	30	5.22 *.3141*	40	5.46 *.3408*
I_2	57	6.42 *.3758*	49	6.10 *.3562*	60	6.31 *.3557*	14	5.81 *.3060*	30	5.78 *.3875*	40	6.01 *.3571*
$\bar{C}$	58	7.03 *.3911*	50	6.85 *.3421*	60	7.16 *.2963*	14	6.59 *.4383*	30	6.48 *.3821*	40	6.82 *.4166*
P_1	58	7.46 *.4628*	50	7.25 *.3883*	60	7.27 *.4033*	14	6.92 *.4644*	30	7.00 *.3557*	40	7.44 *.4941*
P_2	51	7.45 *.5178*	50	7.18 *.4333*	60	7.33 *.5019*	14	6.74 *.5184*	26	7.07 *.5105*	40	7.60 *.6129*
M_1	58	11.68 *.6955*	50	11.27 *.4195*	60	11.32 *.5131*	14	10.80 *.5478*	30	10.74 *.5427*	40	11.47 *.5835*
M_2	43	11.29 *.6267*	50	10.42 *.5225*	60	10.91 *.5452*	14	10.14 *.6010*	22	10.25 *.5527*	22	10.89 *.5875*

similar coefficients of variation to those reported by Barrett et al., but still the coefficient for the mandibular first molars is somewhat larger than that for the mandibular second molars.

Compared with the other five populations listed in Table 15, Aborigines show relatively large size variability, both in males and females; and Caucasians and American Negroes also show larger coefficients than the Mongoloid populations. This result probably tells that the coefficients of variation do not reflect the size of teeth in respective populations.

It is of interest to observe mean values of coefficients of variation in the populations presented here. As stated by Barrett et al., the coefficients for the maxillary lateral incisors are the largest and those for the first molars the smallest, being particularly small in the maxillary first molars. Next to the first molars, the maxillary and mandibular canines also show relatively small size variability.

Within each morphological tooth group, the distal teeth usually show greater variability than the mesial teeth to a more or less extent. The only exception is the mandibular

Table 11. Mean Mesiodistal Crown Diameters in the Permanent Dentition Reported by Previous Authors

Sex	Tooth	Aborigine* (Campbell, '25)	Aborigine (Barrett et al., '63)	Aleut (Moorrees, '57)	Javanese (Mijsberg, '31)	Lapp (Selmer-Olsen, '49)	Swede (Seipel, '46)	Tristanite (Thomsen, '55)
Male	I^1	9.4	9.35	8.45	8.5	8.37	8.84	8.78
	I^2	6.9	7.65	7.29	7.0	6.84	6.81	6.74
	C	8.4	8.31	8.03	8.0	7.74	8.10	7.93
	P^1	7.8	7.69	7.15	7.5	6.75	7.18	6.96
	P^2	7.2	7.19	6.65	7.0	6.45	6.97	6.64
	M^1	11.4	11.34	10.37	10.8	10.23	10.69	10.69
	M^2	10.9	10.70	10.00	10.0	9.34	10.47	10.03
	I$_1$	6.0	5.87	5.23	5.5	5.36	5.51	5.54
	I$_2$	6.7	6.60	6.09	6.2	5.98	6.13	6.08
	C̄	7.6	7.49	7.20	7.2	6.82	7.12	7.15
	P$_1$	7.6	7.49	7.01	7.3	6.72	7.27	7.07
	P$_2$	7.7	7.56	7.17	7.3	6.74	7.41	7.21
	M$_1$	12.3	12.04	11.56	11.5	10.95	11.24	11.22
	M$_2$	12.5	11.45	11.19	10.9	10.51	11.15	10.77
Female	I^1		9.00	8.07	8.2	8.34	8.62	8.60
	I^2		7.34	7.08	6.7	6.70	6.64	6.68
	C		7.95	7.67	7.7	7.47	7.73	7.74
	P$_1$		7.53	6.96	7.3	6.55	7.04	7.02
	P$_2$		7.01	6.61	6.9	6.32	6.85	6.59
	M^1		10.92	10.05	10.5	9.93	10.47	10.45
	M^2		10.31	9.84	9.6	8.93	10.05	9.78
	I$_1$		5.68	5.08	5.4	5.22	5.42	5.49
	I$_2$		6.36	5.90	6.1	5.85	5.94	6.08
	C̄		7.01	6.71	6.8	6.50	6.69	6.87
	P$_1$		7.36	6.85	7.1	6.59	7.16	7.10
	P$_2$		7.31	7.02	7.1	6.59	7.21	7.13
	M$_1$		11.62	11.20	11.2	10.64	10.98	11.01
	M$_2$		11.07	11.16	10.4	10.06	10.70	10.51

* Both sexes seem to be combined.

incisors in which the lateral teeth show considerably smaller size variability in comparison with the mesial teeth. Several authors such as Butler (1939), Dahlberg (1945, 49) and Moorrees (1957) have drawn attention to the fact that in general tooth size and morphology are more stable in the mesial teeth than in the distal teeth within each tooth group, but here again the reverse is true for the mandibular incisor group. In addition, the canines seem to be relatively stable in comparison with the teeth which belong to the other tooth groups. The general trend shown by coefficients of variation is quite compatible with observations pointed out by previous authors.

4. Tooth Crown Measurements

Table 12. T-test for Difference in Mean Mesiodistal Crown Diameters between Aborigines and Other Populations

Sex	Tooth	Japanese	Pima	Ainu	Caucasian	Am. Negro
Male	I^1	—		—	—	
	I^2	—		—	—	—
	C	—	+	—	—	
	P^1	—		—	—	
	P^2	—	+	—	—	
	M^1	—	—	—	—	—
	M^2	—	—	—	—	—
	I$_1$	—		—	—	—
	I$_2$	—	+	—	—	—
	C̄	—	+	—	—	
	P$_1$	—		—	—	+
	P$_2$	—		—	—	
	M$_1$	—		—	—	
	M$_2$	—		—	—	
Female	I^1	—	—	—	—	—
	I^2	—		—	—	—
	C	—	+	—	—	
	P^1	—	—	—	—	—
	P^2	—		—	—	
	M^1	—	—	—	—	—
	M^2	—	—	—	—	—
	I$_1$	—		—	—	—
	I$_2$	—		—	—	—
	C̄	—	+	—	—	
	P$_1$	—	—	—	—	
	P$_2$	—		—	—	
	M$_1$	—	—	—	—	—
	M$_2$	—	—	—	—	

4.1.3. Depth of Lingual Fossa in the Permanent Maxillary Central Incisors

Since Hrdlička (1920) has drawn attention to the anthropological importance of the shovel-shaped teeth, a number of studies of this character have been carried out in regard to between-population differences, genetics, evolutionary significance, morphogenesis, etc. Most of these works employed non-metrical method of classification, so that the expression of the shovel-shaping was usually classified into a few discrete categories and analysed in the same manner as blood groups, ear wax pattern, and so forth.

However, the expression of the shovel-shaping is continuously distributed and hence it might be rather inappropriate to apply the analytical methods for discrete traits to this character. Based on this view, Dahlberg and Mikkelsen (1949) made direct measurements of the shovel-shaped character. They applied this method to the incisors of Pima

Table 13. Comparison between Mean Mesiodistal Crown Diameters of Aborigines and Grand Mean of Five Populations (Permanent Dentition)

Sex	Tooth	Aborigine (1)	Grand Mean (2)	Ratio (1)/(2)%
Male	I^1	9.25	8.77	105.47
	I^2	7.53	7.15	105.31
	C	8.26	8.19	100.85
	P^1	7.70	7.39	104.19
	P^2	7.12	6.97	102.15
	M^1	11.31	10.78	104.92
	M^2	10.96	10.02	109.38
	I$_1$	5.78	5.59	103.40
	I$_2$	6.48	6.23	104.01
	C̄	7.42	7.24	102.49
	P$_1$	7.53	7.35	102.45
	P$_2$	7.63	7.32	104.23
	M$_1$	11.99	11.55	103.81
	M$_2$	11.55	10.96	105.38
Female	I^1	9.10	8.55	106.43
	I^2	7.46	6.99	106.72
	C	8.01	7.82	102.43
	P^1	7.64	7.23	105.67
	P^2	7.17	6.83	104.98
	M^1	11.14	10.43	106.81
	M^2	10.76	9.75	110.36
	I$_1$	5.67	5.41	104.81
	I$_2$	6.42	6.00	107.00
	C̄	7.03	6.78	103.69
	P$_1$	7.46	7.18	103.90
	P$_2$	7.45	7.18	103.76
	M$_1$	11.68	11.12	105.04
	M$_2$	11.29	10.52	107.32

Indians using a modified Bowley gauge. The same method was also employed by Carbonell (1963) but she attached importance rather to the ordinary method in her discussions.

Because of morphological delicacy, however, the measuring instruments should be carefully designed to measure depth of the lingual fossa in the incisors. In 1970, Hanihara et al. developed a more reliable instrument that allows fairly detailed measurements. This is a dial gauge with a pair of adjustable arms which is accurate to 0.01 mm and reads to the nearest 0.05 mm.

Using this dial gauge, they measured depth of the lingual fossa of the maxillary central incisors and found that 1) this character represented a typical normal distribution so that the ordinary statistical procedures could be applied without any trans-

4. Tooth Crown Measurements

Table 14. Coefficients of Variation (CV) in the Permanent Dentition

Sex	Tooth	Aborigine	Japanese	Pima	Ainu	Am. Caucasian	Am. Negro	Total
Male	I^1	6.38	5.26	4.20	5.07	7.48	6.01	5.73
	I^2	7.49	7.37	4.80	5.10	8.90	9.15	7.14
	C	6.37	4.42	5.48	4.08	5.74	5.34	5.24
	P^1	6.6	5.71	5.88	5.49	6.14	6.00	5.97
	P^2	6.46	4.93	6.00	5.06	7.49	7.19	6.19
	M^1	4.57	4.75	4.90	4.36	5.56	5.46	4.93
	M^2	5.61	5.08	5.06	6.13	5.89	6.03	5.63
	I_1	7.17	6.53	7.27	4.85	7.73	5.82	6.56
	I_2	6.37	5.63	5.86	5.58	7.86	6.23	6.26
	$\bar{C}$	6.58	5.32	5.12	4.54	6.49	7.05	5.85
	P_1	7.93	5.12	5.57	4.42	5.56	6.09	5.78
	P_2	7.34	5.08	7.10	4.91	6.90	7.49	6.47
	M_1	7.07	3.97	4.19	4.62	5.81	5.43	5.18
	M_2	5.76	6.59	4.76	6.71	6.68	6.59	6.18
Total		6.55	5.41	5.44	5.07	6.73	6.42	
Female	I^1	6.43	5.37	4.90	5.26	6.23	4.60	5.47
	I^2	9.02	7.57	6.06	10.23	8.60	7.03	8.09
	C	6.18	5.84	4.07	5.87	4.56	5.08	5.27
	P^1	5.50	5.45	5.39	5.06	5.81	6.33	5.61
	P^2	6.50	5.73	5.79	8.08	6.93	5.64	6.45
	M^1	5.31	4.25	4.51	4.40	4.37	5.81	4.78
	M^2	6.47	4.56	4.64	7.71	4.58	4.70	5.44
	I_1	7.08	5.60	5.26	6.66	6.02	6.24	6.14
	I_2	5.85	5.84	5.64	5.27	6.70	5.94	5.87
	$\bar{C}$	5.24	4.99	4.14	6.65	5.90	6.11	5.51
	P_1	6.20	5.36	5.55	6.71	5.08	6.64	5.92
	P_2	6.95	6.03	6.85	7.69	7.22	8.06	7.13
	M_1	5.95	3.72	4.53	5.07	5.05	5.09	4.90
	M_2	5.55	5.01	5.00	5.93	5.39	5.39	5.38
Total		6.30	5.39	5.17	6.47	5.89	5.9	

formation of the original data; 2) there was a high correlation between the measurements and the categories of classification which had been used by previous authors; and 3) there was no significant sex difference in mean values of this measurement.

Based on such findings, they compared average values among Japanese, American Caucasians, Pima Indians and American Negroes, and found considerable differences which paralleled the results obtained by the usual method of classification.

Following this method, the present author measured depth of the lingual fossa of the maxillary central incisors in Aborigines as a measure of the shovel-shaping, and compared with those of several other populations. It is quite evident from Table 15 that Pimas represent the largest mean values and are followed by Japanese and Ainu. On the other hand, Caucasians show the smallest mean value among the six populations

Table 15. Depth of Lingual Fossa in the Upper Central Incisors (Both Sexes Combined)

Population	No. of Samples	Mean (in mm)	Variance
Aborigine	160	0.81	0.0679
Japanese	444	0.99*	0.1117
Pima	216	1.21*	0.1198
Ainu	46	0.87	0.1595
Caucasian	59	0.41*	0.0717
Am. Negro	80	0.53*	0.0505

* Difference from the Aborigines is significant at the 1% level.

compared and American Negroes are the next smallest. These results are almost completely compatible with those obtained through traditional observation method of the shovel-shaped character.

Among the five populations, Aborigines represent an intermediate mean value between the Mongoloids and the Caucasians as well as the American Negroes. On the other hand, difference between Aborigines and Ainu is small and statistically insignificant, so that the two populations are quite similar to each other as far as this particular trait is concerned.

The mean value of this trait in American Negroes is close to that of Caucasians, but probably it has been affected by admixture with Caucasians to some extent. According to Carbonell (1963), frequencies of shovel-shaped maxillary central incisors are 21.1% in Anglo-Saxons, 34.3% in Bantu and 92.7% in Asian Mongoloids. These data seem to suggest that the shovel-shaping in Negroes might be much closer to Caucasians than to Mongoloids, even if full-blood Negroes were observed.

4.2. Sex Difference in Mesiodistal Crown Diameters as a Whole

In order to compare the sex difference in terms of overall size of dentition among different populations, Hanihara (1974) computed Mahalanobis' generalized distances between male and female groups using mesiodistal crown diameters in I^1, $\underline{C}$, P^2, M^2, I_2, P_1, M_1 and M_2. This calculation was based on a pooled dispersion matrix of five populations, Aborigines, Japanese, Pimas, Caucasians and American Negroes, so that the distances between male and female groups were directly compared in a common multi-dimensional space.

Table 16. Generalized Distance between Males and Females Based on Mesiodistal Crown Diameters

Population	D^2	Probability
Aborigine	0.6850	$p<0.01$
Japanese	0.6285	$p<0.01$
Pima	1.8196	$p<0.01$
Caucasian	1.5410	$p<0.01$
Am. Negro	1.6776	$p<0.01$

4. Tooth Crown Measurements

Table 17. Factor Loadings after Varimax Rotation

Tooth	Factor 1	Factor 2
I^1	0.1373	0.8264
C	0.2007	0.5334
P^2	0.1658	0.2632
M^2	0.3811	0.1261
I$_2$	0.2237	0.8332
P$_1$	0.2754	0.1629
M$_1$	0.8191	0.2760
M$_2$	0.8198	0.1212

Table 16 shows that all the distances are statistically significant under the 1% level. However, between-sex distances are somewhat different among the populations involved; namely, the distances are evidently smaller in some populations than in the others. This shows quite likely that between-sex differences in overall tooth size, not in individual tooth size, are much smaller in Aborigines and Japanese than in Pimas, Caucasians and American Negroes.

Hanihara further goes to compute canonical variates based on the generalized distance using Rao's method (1952). The purpose of this procedure is to make relationship between male and female groups more evident. The generalized distances shown in Table 16 are those in the nine-dimensional space, because ten groups in total are compared in combination so that the location of each group in such a space is hardly recognized in reality. However, it is possible to project all the groups to a space of reduced dimensions by using canonical variates.

In the present case, if the first and second canonical variates are taken into account, they may contain about 77% of the total informations which could be obtained from the samples. This means that a graph drawn on the basis of two sets of canonical

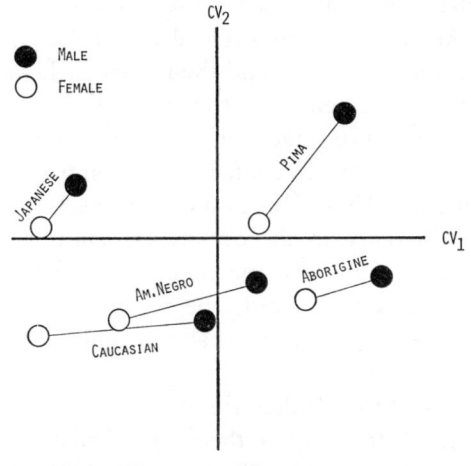

Figure 1. Between-Sex Difference in Mesiodistal Crown Diameters as Shown by Canonical Variates I and II

variates may be equivalent to a projection of ten groups to a two-dimensional space with a loss of about 23% of total variance (Figure 1).

The results seem to be quite suggestive. In the first place, the distances between males and females are relatively small in Japanese and Aborigines, and larger in the other three populations. This agrees quite well with the results obtained from the direct comparison of the generalized distances. Secondly, it may be realized that the inclination of the lines connecting male and female groups varies from population to population; namely, the inclination is relatively steep in Japanese and Pimas, but much more gentle in the other populations. In other words, between-sex difference is almost the same in both directions of the first and second canonical variates in the former two populations, but the difference is particularly large in the direction of the first canonical variates in the latter populations. This seems to mean that the between-sex difference is not the same in all the populations, because the two sets of canonical variates represent different factors which concern the tooth crown size, and they are uncorrelated with each other.

In the second step of this study, Hanihara carried out factor analysis of the mesiodistal crown measurements to interpret the meanings of the first and second canonical variates. Table 17 shows factor loadings after orthogonal rotation using varimax method. Factor 1 represents significantly higher correlation with the mandibular molars, and less but still significant correlation with the maxillary molars. On the other hand, Factor 2 shows higher correlation with the incisors, and somewhat less with the maxillary canine.

Based on these results, it is quite evident that the size of molars largely contributes to the Factor 1, and that of incisors to the Factor 2. On the other hand, the premolars show almost no correlation with either Factor 1 or Factor 2. This seems to mean that the premolars could be represented by some other factors.

Since the canonical variates and the factor loadings have been calculated from the same samples, rates of contribution to the total variance are likely to parallel each other, and this supposition is proved by comparing a graph drawn from the canonical variates on one hand, with that from mean factor scores on the other. The graphs, which are quite similar to each other, show that the between-sex difference is particularly large in size of the molars and relatively small in that of the incisors as well as the canines in Aborigines, Caucasians and American Negroes. On the other hand, almost the same extent of difference is shown by the front teeth and the molars in Japanese and Pimas.

As a whole, Aboriginal permanent dentition is similar to Japanese in its relatively small between-sex difference, but to Caucasians and American Negroes in its pattern of difference to which the molars largely contribute in comparison with the front teeth. Pimas are quite different from Aborigines in both aspects.

In regard to the sex difference in the deciduous dentition, no calculation of generalized distance was carried out because the numbers of teeth were so small in some populations that reliable results could hardly be obtained. Instead of this, the present author compared male and female groups using a simple method to guess general trends of between-sex difference.

The method employed is 1) to calculate simple sum of mean mesiodistal crown diameters in each group, and 2) to compare them by calculating the 'sex ratio' between male and female groups, or the percentage of the sum of female group to that of male group.

Table 18. Sex Ratio of Simple Sums of Mean Mesiodistal Crown Diameters in the Deciduous Dentition

Population	Simple Sum Male	Simple Sum Female	Sex Ratio (Female/Male %)
Aborigine	73.26	72.56	99.04
Japanese	69.08	67.89	98.28
Pima	70.81	69.58	98.26
Caucasian	66.02	65.59	99.35
Am. Negro	67.50	68.25	101.11 (?)

Table 18 shows that the 'sex ratio' distributes within a very narrow range of percentages. This means probably that the between-sex difference varies little from population to population. The simple sums for American Negroes are larger in female group than in male group so that the 'sex ratio' reaches more than 100%. However, this result may be caused by the very small number of front teeth, most of which were replaced by permanent teeth.

However, it is of interest to note that Aborigines show relatively small between-sex difference compared with Japanese and Pimas. This trend is quite similar to that of the permanent dentition.

Although this simple method of comparison does not reveal rates of contribution of each factor which controls general size of the deciduous dentition, comparison of mean mesiodistal crown diameters in male and female groups may show some trends of contribution of each tooth to the between-sex difference.

In the deciduous incisors and canines, the mean values of the female group are almost the same as or a little bit smaller than those of the male group. However discrepancies between the sexes are somewhat larger in the deciduous molars. This trend is shown by the fact that, in the deciduous molars, the mean values for females amount to 92–98% of those for males. On the other hand, the ratios between male and female groups are almost equal, being around 98%, in every deciduous tooth in Japanese.

These results are likely to show that the pattern of sex difference is somewhat different between Aborigines and Japanese. Namely, contribution of the deciduous molars to the sex difference is particularly large in Aborigines, while almost the same as that of the deciduous incisors and canines in Japanese. This trend is quite similar to that of the permanent dentition described above, and suggests that, among different populations, some discrepancies in pattern of contribution of each tooth or tooth group to between-sex difference exist in both permanent and deciduous dentitions.

4.3. Comparison of Mesiodistal Crown Diameters between Yuendumu and Queensland Materials

Based on osteological as well as somatological data, homogeneity or heterogeneity of Aborigines has been discussed by many previous authors. As is well-known, Tindale and Birdsell (1941) and Birdsell (1950) proposed the so-called trihybrid theory on the

Table 19. Comparison of Mesiodistal Diameters in Molar Crowns between Yuendumu and Queensland Aborigines

Sex	Tooth	Yuendumu N	Yuendumu Mean	Yuendumu SD	Queensland N	Queensland Mean	Queensland SD	Value of t
Male	M^1	79	11.37	0.5167	21	11.30	0.4706	0.0794
	M^2	59	10.96	0.6152	23	10.83	0.6419	0.8813
	M^3	30	10.30	0.9133	19	9.99	0.5496	1.3411
	M_1	78	11.99	0.8479	15	12.09	0.4964	0.4341
	M_2	59	11.55	0.6657	17	11.96	0.7035	2.2306*
	M_3	28	11.76	0.9805	14	12.04	1.3001	0.7725
Female	M^1	57	11.14	0.5911	17	11.09	0.6264	0.3310
	M^2	50	10.76	0.6967	20	10.45	0.8556	1.5229
	M^3	25	10.05	0.8176	14	9.84	0.7977	0.7993
	M_1	58	11.68	0.6955	12	11.54	0.7012	0.6425
	M_2	43	11.29	0.6267	15	11.37	0.9969	0.3281
	M_3	24	11.29	0.7973	13	11.27	0.7962	0.0911

* Between-group difference is significant under the 5% level.

basis of geographical variation of several somatological traits appearing in Aborigines. On the other hand, Howells (1937), Abbie (1951, 1968, 1969), Macintosh (1963), Yamaguchi (1967), etc. stressed importance of homogeneity of this population on the basis of evidence including osteological findings.

As to the dental traits of the Aborigines, as far as the present author knows, almost no comparative studies in regard to the geographical variation has been carried out on this population. Very fortunately the author had an opportunity, at the Department of Anatomy, the University of Sydney, to observe skulls derived from Queensland which were in the collections of the Australian Museum in Sydney. Because of limited time, only a few measurements on skulls as well as the maxillary and mandibular molars were carried out.

In this section, comparison of mesiodistal diameters of the molar crowns between Yuendumu and Queensland materials will be made to show whether the between-group difference is significant or insignificant.

One can see from Table 19 that the differences in mesiodistal crown diameters of the molars, both males and females, are insignificant between Yuendumu and Queensland groups, except for the mandibular second molars in males. The results seem to show that at least the molar crown size is almost identical in the two groups which settled far from each other.

In addition, the Yuendumu group is a little bit larger than the Queensland group in M^1, M^2 and M^3 in males, and in M^1, M^2, M^3, M_1 and M_3 in females. This seems to show that the between-group difference fluctuates at random in the molar region, and, in turn, there seems to be no definite pattern in the difference between the two groups. This fact may prove the supposition that the minor difference between the two groups occurred as an accidental fluctuation.

According to Birdsell (1950), phenotypic frequencies as well as estimated gene frequencies for tawny hair, for example, are quite different between the central and eastern parts of Australia, being considerably high in the Central Australia and practically absent in Queensland. The evidence obtained from the molar crown size is, as shown above, quite different from that obtained from the hair form.

Although this single example can hardly be extended to overall dental characteristics, similarity in the crown size between the two separated groups of Aborigines should be remembered for future studies.

4.4. Principal Component Analysis

4.4.1. Principal Component Analysis of the Mesiodistal Crown Diameters

Before we enter into comparison of tooth size among different populations on the basis of biological distance, it is of importance to summarize the mesiodistal crown diameters into a small number of new variables that are called principal components, and to compare the populations in terms of these variables.

Hanihara (1974, 1976) carried out factor analysis on the mesiodistal crown diameters of the deciduous dentition, and principal component analysis on those of the permanent dentition.

In regard to the deciduous dentition, he found that the first factor was related to general size of the tooth crown so that this factor was referred to as size factor; the second was a shape factor which contrasts the size of front teeth with the back teeth; and the third was a factor mainly related to the crown size of the deciduous canines. The rates of contribution of these three factors are about 75% in Japanese and 82% in Aborigines.

Next to this, the author computed factor scores based on the factor loadings and summarized deciduous dentition in some different populations as follows: the deciduous dentition of Japanese may be characterized by medium general size, relatively large back teeth compared with the front teeth, and smaller canines; those of Caucasians by smaller general size, relatively smaller molars and moderate size of canines; those of Pimas by medium to larger general size, larger size of incisors and canines; and Aborigines by larger general size, particularly larger size of molars and moderate size of canines in proportion.

On the other hand, applying principal component analysis to mesiodistal crown diameters of the permanent dentition, Hanihara concluded that the first component relates to the size of the premolars, both maxillary and mandibular; the second to that of the maxillary lateral incisor which shows somewhat different behavior from the other three incisors; the third to the maxillary and mandibular molar size; the fourth to the size of the maxillary and mandibular canines; and the fifth to the size of the maxillary central incisor and the two mandibular incisors.

In regard to these findings, Lombardi (1975) found almost the same components on the basis of 66 Mexican skulls, although proportions of the total variance in each component were somewhat different from those found by Hanihara.

As in the study on deciduous dentition, Hanihara went further to compute factor scores using rotated factor loadings, and compared mean factor scores in each popula-

Table 20. Pooled Correlation Matrix for Mesiodistal Crown Diameters in Deciduous and Permanent Dentitions

1.00																											
.75	1.00																										
.62	.59	1.00																									
.66	.55	.55	1.00																								
.55	.56	.50	.78	1.00																							
.79	.61	.41	.80	.66	1.00																						
.83	.72	.51	.71	.69	.85	1.00																					
.65	.58	.69	.55	.58	.50	.65	1.00																				
.51	.55	.57	.78	.79	.55	.55	.64	1.00																			
.47	.59	.39	.66	.84	.65	.54	.60	.81	1.00																		
.60	.40	.36	.49	.35	.61	.69	.55	.41	.31	1.00																	
.54	.32	.44	.36	.14	.40	.34	.55	.35	.24	.48	1.00																
.45	.44	.42	.42	.42	.60	.42	.51	.43	.39	.47	.41	1.00															
.66	.47	.34	.45	.44	.53	.48	.58	.54	.44	.46	.36	.52	1.00														
.68	.63	.46	.55	.58	.72	.71	.70	.65	.63	.41	.24	.40	.71	1.00													
.41	.33	.51	.59	.65	.39	.45	.70	.66	.64	.43	.28	.41	.54	.59	1.00												
.69	.37	.48	.50	.55	.42	.72	.64	.59	.59	.37	.27	.27	.44	.49	.62	1.00											
.53	.36	.34	.46	.40	.36	.57	.50	.42	.37	.59	.45	.43	.41	.43	.46	.39	1.00										
.31	.38	.26	.38	.34	.21	.46	.50	.40	.41	.60	.46	.52	.46	.41	.43	.28	.72	1.00									
.46	.36	.44	.37	.36	.43	.44	.60	.39	.51	.41	.39	.67	.56	.45	.47	.28	.53	.62	1.00								
.56	.39	.40	.51	.45	.55	.49	.59	.60	.56	.37	.34	.44	.75	.63	.55	.47	.40	.42	.52	1.00							
.36	.34	.45	.42	.36	.25	.32	.58	.53	.47	.39	.27	.43	.66	.68	.60	.46	.44	.42	.50	.70	1.00						
.44	.42	.34	.57	.52	.39	.52	.61	.65	.59	.34	.23	.38	.46	.48	.62	.48	.41	.42	.43	.47	.52	1.00					
.66	.62	.54	.55	.64	.75	.68	.62	.67	.66	.31	.24	.34	.47	.42	.59	.56	.39	.35	.37	.44	.52	.60	1.00				

The variables are arranged in order of maxillary and mandibular deciduous teeth, and maxillary and mandibular permanent teeth (the third molars excluded).

tion studied. The results were summarized as follows: Aborigines are one of the groups with the largest overall tooth size, but their premolars and canines are relatively small and the molars are very large in comparison with the other teeth; Japanese are intermediate in general tooth size but the canines are relatively large; the Ainu dentition belongs to the group with the smallest overall tooth size among the six populations compared, especially the maxillary lateral incisor and the canines being small but the molars relatively large; Caucasians are very small in premolar, molar and incisor size but the maxillary lateral incisor and canines are a little bit larger; Pima Indians, in general, show the largest tooth size, particularly the size of the canines being the largest among the populations under consideration; and the American Negroes again show larger overall tooth size but the maxillary lateral incisor and the canines are somewhat smaller in a relative sense.

As cited above, comparison of populations using factor scores is useful because they clearly show relative quantities of main factors which largely control the size of dentition. Using this method, the size and shape of the dentition may be more clearly represented than in direct comparison of size of each tooth.

In the papers cited above, Hanihara analysed deciduous and permanent dentitions separately since the data of both dentitions were taken from different individuals in most of the populations compared. However, part of the dental casts of deciduous and permanent dentition from the Aborigines were derived from the same individuals who had been studied continuously for a considerably long time.

Of 116 male and 104 female Aborigines, 54 and 32 individuals provide dental casts of deciduous and permanent dentitions, if not the full set of the teeth. Using mesiodistal crown diameters from these individuals, a correlation matrix which covers both deciduous and permanent dentitions was computed. In this procedure the correlation matrices were computed for males and females separately and then they were pooled together, since the numbers of individuals were small if males and females were treated separately. The purpose of this analysis is to extract principal components from a multi-dimensional space which is common to the deciduous and permanent dentitions, and to compare the populations in terms of principal components of dental measurements.

Table 20 gives the pooled correlation matrix for mesiodistal crown diameters of deciduous and permanent dentitions, with the exception of the maxillary and mandibular third molars. The first ten eigenvalues computed from the above matrix as well as their cumulative proportions of total variance are shown in Table 21.

It is evident from the table that the first five eigenvalues amount to 1.0 or more so that the first five principal components may be significant, and their cumulative proportion of the total variance is 76.46%.

For the next step of the analysis, we should interpret each component through factor loadings which represent correlation coefficients between principal components and original variables. Based on the correlation matrix, factor loadings have been obtained as shown in Table 22. All the factor loadings for the first component show positive values, ranging from 0.5072 to 0.8436, so that this component appears to be related to overall size of dentition including deciduous and permanent teeth. This means that whenever the tooth or teeth become larger the value of the first principal component also becomes larger, and vice versa.

Table 21. First Ten Eigenvalues and Cumulative Proportion of Total Variance

Order of Eigenvalue	Eigenvalue	Cumulative Proportion of Total Variance
1	12.674	0.5281
2	1.959	0.6097
3	1.600	0.6764
4	1.111	0.7227
5	1.005	0.7646
6	0.890	0.8016
7	0.694	0.8306
8	0.605	0.8558
9	0.580	0.8800
10	0.484	0.9001

Table 22. Factor Loadings for the First Five Principal Components

Tooth	Fac. 1	Fac. 2	Fac. 3	Fac. 4	Fac. 5
di^1	.8215	.0604	−.4189	.2358	.1639
di^2	.7171	.1739	−.3081	.1162	.0060
$d\underline{c}$	.6685	.0542	−.0982	.0235	.5103
dm^1	.7957	.2536	−.1173	−.1639	−.1291
dm^2	.7725	.4158	.0495	−.2299	−.1884
di_1	.7845	.2256	−.4265	.1742	−.3100
di_2	.8339	.1477	−.3992	−.0383	−.0453
$d\bar{c}$	.8436	−.0956	.0804	−.0048	.3155
dm_1	.8197	.2408	.2271	−.1514	−.0244
dm_2	.7728	.3455	.2097	−.1718	−.1900
I^1	.6534	−.3752	−.3287	−.1320	−.0797
I^2	.5072	−.4402	−.2900	−.0409	.3445
$\underline{C}$	.6331	−.3538	−.0724	.0406	−.2514
P^1	.7318	−.2084	.1781	.4511	−.1305
P^2	.7958	.0745	.0865	.3509	−.1269
M^1	.7458	.0491	.4118	−.1750	.1311
M^2	.6950	.2287	.0647	−.0544	.3545
I_1	.6416	−.4125	−.0786	−.3325	−.0343
I_2	.6015	−.5507	.0678	−.3551	−.1663
$\bar{C}$	.6570	−.4805	.0818	−.0033	−.1242
P_1	.7261	−.1120	.2818	.3763	−.0880
P_2	.6665	−.2000	.5074	.2565	.0944
M_1	.6872	.0901	.3090	−.2172	−.0211
M_2	.7578	.3125	−.0075	−.0714	.0761

In regard to the second through the fifth components, the factor loadings take either plus or minus signs. This fact clearly shows that these components are, to a more or less extent, related to the shape component of dental measurements and contrast the

4. Tooth Crown Measurements

size of certain teeth with that of the other teeth. However, the absolute values of the factor loadings are generally much smaller than those for the first principal components, so that the interpretation is not easy.

Attending to the factor loadings showing the value of 0.4 or over, those for dm^2, I^2, I_1, I_2 and $\bar{C}$ may be picked up for the second principal component, and the signs are minus except for that of dm^2. From this fact it may be supposed that this component mainly relates to size of the permanent incisors and canines in one direction, and the deciduous maxillary second molars in another.

In regard to the third principal component, factor loadings for di^1 and di_1 show the values greater than 0.4 with minus signs, and those for M^1 and P_2 with plus signs. The fourth principal component correlates only with P^1, and the fifth only with $d\underline{c}$.

As a result, interpretation of each principal component is quite difficult except for the first component, because absolute values of factor loadings are generally small and weighting for each tooth does not vary in a regular way.

In order to make interpretations more easy, the varimax rotation method was applied on the original matrix of factor loadings (Table 23). As easily seen, it is evident that the interpretation after rotation is much easier than that before rotation.

Table 23. Rotated Factor Loadings for the First Five Principal Components

Tooth	Fac. 1	Fac. 2	Fac. 3	Fac. 4	Fac. 5
di^1	.1736	−.1409	−.7164	.3035	.3022
di^2	.3332	−.1753	−.3898	.1907	.0801
$d\underline{c}$	.2675	.0011	−.0995	.1386	.5347
dm^1	.7297	−.1567	−.4237	.1585	.2547
dm^2	.8197	−.1186	−.2906	.1280	−.0035
di_1	.4707	.0007	−.8007	.2034	.1039
di_2	.3270	−.3323	−.7466	.1460	.0432
$d\bar{c}$	.3079	−.2658	−.1715	.3719	.3649
dm_1	.7778	−.1466	−.1030	.3209	.2069
dm_2	.8171	−.1479	−.1546	.2744	−.0044
I^1	.0949	−.5675	−.5332	.1521	.2695
I^2	.0572	−.3050	−.1959	.1304	.8190
$\underline{C}$	.2088	−.2143	−.2234	.2201	.1732
P^1	.1508	−.1707	−.3008	.7780	.0797
P^2	.3658	−.1883	−.3567	.6857	.0173
M^1	.5261	−.2212	−.0008	.3706	.1450
M^2	.2964	−.1196	−.3704	.2541	.1490
I_1	.1722	−.7896	−.2170	.1655	.1624
I_2	.1902	−.8527	−.0042	.2092	.1020
$\bar{C}$	.1187	−.3978	−.0925	.3291	.1605
P_1	.3052	−.1081	−.2085	.7684	.1637
P_2	.1985	−.2204	.0916	.7508	.0764
M_1	.4775	−.2682	−0.610	.2461	−.0887
M_2	.4539	−.0565	−.3384	.1364	−.0489

The first principal component is highly correlated with the size of dm^1, dm^2, dm$_1$ and dm$_2$, so that it seems to relate to the size of the deciduous maxillary and mandibular molars. The second component relates with I$_1$ and I$_2$, and a little less with I^1, showing clearly that this component represents size of the permanent maxillary and mandibular incisors with the exception of the maxillary second incisor which shows somewhat different behavior from the remaining incisors. The third component represents size of di^1, di$_1$ and di$_2$; accordingly it highly correlates with the deciduous incisors except for the deciduous maxillary second incisor. The fourth component shows high correlation with size of P^1, P$_1$ and P$_2$, and a little less with P^2. The results appear to mean that this component closely relates to the permanent premolars, both maxillary and mandibular. Finally, the fifth component correlates only with the permanent maxillary lateral incisor.

As already described, the five principal components above mentioned have variances which equal or exceed 1.0 and explain 76.46% of total variance in combination. However, they do not represent all the teeth under consideration. This means that the other teeth may be related to the sixth or later principal components. Although these components are statistically less significant, it is of interest to analyse what they mean.

Table 24. Rotated Factor Loadings for the Sixth through Eighth Principal Components

Tooth	Fac. 6	Fac. 7	Fac. 8
di^1	−.0876	.3512	.2807
di^2	−.1170	.7597	.0323
dc	−.1977	.5347	.3840
dm^1	−.0970	.0628	.1127
dm^2	−.1090	.1859	.2066
di$_1$	−.3125	.1301	.0041
di$_2$	−.0530	.2846	.3109
dc̄	−.2123	.3112	.4745
dm$_1$	−.1154	.1614	.2367
dm$_2$	−.0900	.1797	.1772
I^1	−.2165	−.0637	.1348
I^2	−.1718	.0484	.0263
C	−.7891	.0970	.0202
P^1	−.2587	.0861	.1206
P^2	−.0012	.3283	.0719
M^1	−.1670	−.0413	.5447
M^2	.1226	.0402	.7132
I$_1$	−.0900	.0796	.1835
I$_2$	−.2624	.1186	.0474
C̄	−.6692	.1154	.1560
P$_1$	−.1750	−.0103	.1330
P$_2$	−.1734	.1311	.3406
M$_1$	−.2309	.0923	.4877
M$_2$	−.2370	.3643	.5121

4. Tooth Crown Measurements

Table 25. Communalities for Each Tooth Computed by the Method of Factor Analysis

Tooth	Communality
di^1	0.9564
di^2	0.9283
$d\underline{c}$	0.8591
dm^1	0.8526
dm^2	0.8759
di_1	0.9999
di_2	0.9784
$d\bar{c}$	0.8334
dm_1	0.8782
dm_2	0.8604
I^1	0.7803
I^2	0.8549
$\underline{C}$	0.8504
P^1	0.8430
P^2	0.8799
M^1	0.8104
M^2	0.8515
I_1	0.8020
I_2	0.9025
$\bar{C}$	0.8003
P_1	0.8140
P_2	0.8291
M_1	0.6718
M_2	0.7959

According to the rotated factor loadings shown in Table 24, the sixth principal component highly correlates with the permanent maxillary canine and a little less with the permanent mandibular canine; the seventh with the deciduous maxillary lateral incisor; and the eighth with the permanent maxillary second molar and with the other permanent molars in less degree. Thus all the teeth under consideration, except for the deciduous canines, may be summarized into the eight principal components as tabulated in Table 24.

Among these components, it is of particular interest to note that the deciduous maxillary lateral incisor is closely related to the seventh component. Although this tooth does not show a large variability such as that shown by the permanent maxillary lateral incisor, the result seems to mean that this particular tooth has a variance which is more or less independent of those of the other teeth. More detailed studies on this problem should be done in relation to reduction of the human dentition.

It should be also noted here that the principal components with larger eigenvalues, or variances, are not related to the permanent molars and canines which are generally regarded as the teeth showing larger variances than the other teeth. This fact might be resulted from the statistical procedures in which the analysis started from the correlation matrix, or the variance-covariance matrix, based on the standardized data with the mean of 0.0 and the variance of 1.0. This procedure does not represent the absolute size of variances but their relative size. Accordingly, the principal components are extracted in order from those having relatively larger variances regardless of size of the original means and variances.

Secondly, it is noteworthy that the principal components for the deciduous and permanent teeth have been extracted separately. For the first impression of the present author, it was supposed that each group of the deciduous teeth—incisor group, canine group and molar group—might have been combined into respective components together with the corresponding groups of the permanent dentition. The results such as those mentioned above are, however, opposed to this supposition, and suggest that the deciduous and permanent dentitions might be controlled by somewhat different factors.

Thirdly, the order of the principal components ranked by means of eigenvalues may be of another interest. The teeth which are largely related with the principal components are, in descending order, the deciduous molars, permanent incisors, deciduous incisors, permanent premolars, permanent maxillary lateral incisors, permanent canines, deciduous maxillary lateral incisors, and permanent molars.

This order corresponds to the order of contribution rates of each variance to the total variance in a relative sense. For instance, the first principal component which largely represents size of the deciduous molars has the largest variance among all the components if the deciduous and permanent dentition are taken into account in combination. Based on this fact, it is of interest to note that, among the five significant principal components, three of these represent the size of incisors, both the permanent and the deciduous. This fact suggests that, at least in the dentition of Aborigines, the incisors have relatively larger variability than the other teeth. This is also proved by the original factor loadings before rotation (see Table 22), in which the second and third principal components have, in absolute values, relatively larger factor loadings for the permanent and deciduous incisors.

Finally, it may be useful to check the communalities for recognizing dependency of each tooth using techniques of factor analysis. As can be seen in Table 25, the teeth with larger values of communalities (those more than 0.9) are the deciduous incisors and the permanent mandibular lateral incisor, and those with smaller communalities (those less than 0.8) are the permanent maxillary central incisor and the mandibular first and second molars.

This means that the size of the former group of teeth are largely dependent on that of the other teeth, and the size of the latter teeth has a more extent of uniqueness than the other.

4.4.2. *Comparison of Populations in Terms of Principal Components of the Mesiodistal Crown Diameters*

Based on the principal component analysis mentioned above, characteristics of tooth crown measurements in different populations may be compared by means of scores calculated from tooth size which was weighted by corresponding factor loadings. To

4. Tooth Crown Measurements

simplify the calculations, mean values for each tooth in each population and rotated factor loadings were used, and, in calculating functions, the factor loadings with absolute value less than 0.7 were omitted from equations. Thus we have the following five equations:

Function 1 $Z_1 = 0.7297(dm^1) + 0.8197(dm^2) + 0.7778(dm_1) + 0.8171(dm_2)$
Function 2 $Z_2 = 0.7896(I_1) + 0.8527(I_2)$
Function 3 $Z_3 = 0.7164(di^1) + 0.8007(di_1) + 0.7466(di_2)$
Function 4 $Z_4 = 0.7780(P^1) + 0.7684(P_1) + 0.7508(P_2)$
Function 5 $Z_5 = 0.8190(I^2)$.

In equations here presented, symbols dm^1, I_1, etc. stand for mean mesiodistal crown diameters for the deciduous maxillary first molar, those of the permanent mandibular first incisor, etc., in each population.

As it is easily recognized, Functions 1 through 5 represent the components which are largely related with the deciduous molars, permanent lower incisors, deciduous incisors, permanent premolars, and permanent maxillary lateral incisors, respectively.

Since the rotated factor loadings used in the above equations are those computed from the correlation matrix for Aborigines, there is no proof that they could be safely extended to the other populations. However, it is quite difficult to obtain both deciduous and permanent dentitions from the same individuals, so the author dares to use them to compare the characteristics of dentition in different populations.

In addition, the author should mention here that the data for the deciduous molars and incisors were obtained from plaster casts stored in the same institutions as those of the permanent dentition, and measurements were made by the present author (Table 26). In Table 27 the mean factor scores calculated by the formulae shown above, their totals in each population and percentages of each score are shown.

First of all, a rough examination shows that the overall size of the teeth involved is the largest in Aborigines and the smallest in Caucasians, the other three populations being in between. The result is quite parallel to those obtained from the deciduous and permanent dentitions separately.

Secondly, based on each score and its percentage of total score, characteristics in each population may be summarized as follows: Aborigines have the largest deciduous incisors and molars in comparison with those of the other populations, but the per-

Table 26. Mean Mesiodistal Crown Diameters in Some Deciduous Dentition (Males)

Tooth	Aborigine	Japanese	Pima	Caucasian	Am. Negro
dm^1	7.62 (63)	7.42 (60)	7.15 (61)	6.96 (28)	7.43 (22)
dm^2	9.77 (64)	9.46 (60)	7.51 (60)	8.81 (28)	9.24 (23)
dm_1	8.50 (62)	8.23 (60)	8.05 (60)	7.71 (24)	8.16 (17)
dm_2	11.10 (63)	10.36 (60)	10.62 (62)	9.70 (25)	10.21 (19)
di^1	7.31 (32)	6.70 (60)	6.86 (51)	6.40 (10)	6.03 (3)
di_1	4.40 (20)	4.16 (60)	4.22 (24)	3.91 (8)	3.87 (3)
di_2	5.00 (35)	4.64 (60)	4.82 (51)	4.62 (8)	4.38 (4)

Numbers in parentheses show the sample size.

Table 27. Mean Factor Scores Weighted by the Rotated Factor Loadings (Males)

Function No.	1	2	3	4	5	Total
Related Teeth	dm^1, dm^2 dm_1, dm_2	I_1, I_2	di^1, di_1 di_2	P^1, P_1 P_2	I^2	
Aborigine	29.25 *38.74*	10.09 *13.36*	12.49 *16.55*	17.51 *23.18*	6.17 *8.17*	75.51
Japanese	28.05 *38.99*	9.65 *13.41*	11.60 *16.11*	16.82 *23.37*	5.84 *8.12*	71.96
Pima	26.31 *36.27*	10.37 *14.30*	11.89 *16.39*	17.67 *24.36*	6.29 *8.67*	72.53
Caucasian	26.22 *38.14*	9.49 *13.81*	11.17 *16.24*	16.44 *23.92*	5.43 *7.90*	68.75
Am. Negro	27.69 *38.64*	9.71 *13.55*	10.69 *14.92*	17.73 *24.74*	5.84 *8.15*	71.66

Figures in italics represent percentages of total score.

manent incisors and premolars do not necessarily show the largest size among the populations under consideration; Japanese carry relatively larger deciduous molars; Pimas have the largest permanent incisors, both in absolute size and in proportion, relatively small deciduous molars and large premolars; Caucasians show the smallest scores in every function and particularly the smallest percentage for the maxillary lateral incisors; and American Negroes carry the smallest deciduous incisors in absolute size and proportion among the five populations.

These results are generally quite similar to those of previous studies by Hanihara, but slightly different in evaluation of contribution of each tooth. This naturally resuls from the difference in original correlation matrices on which the analyses have been based.

4.5. Distance Analysis

4.5.1. *Mahalanobis' Generalized Distance Based on the Mesiodistal Crown Diameters in the Permanent Dentition*

In this section, biological distance between Aborigines and certain other populations is analysed in terms of Mahalanobis' generalized distance, D^2, based on the mesiodistal crown diameters. The generalized distances were computed only for the permanent dentition, both male and female groups.

In computing distances, some additional populations reported by several previous authors were included. However, since no variance-covariance matrix for these additional populations has been given, a pooled dispersion matrices obtained from the populations studied by the author were used. The populations newly included here are Aleuts (Moorrees, 1957), Javanese (Mijsberg, 1931), Norwegian Lapps (Selmer-Olsen, 1949), Swedes (Seipel, 1946), Tristanites (Thomsen, 1955) and North American Whites (Moorrees et al., 1957).

Figures 2 and 3 illustrate generalized distances between Aborigines and other popula-

4. Tooth Crown Measurements

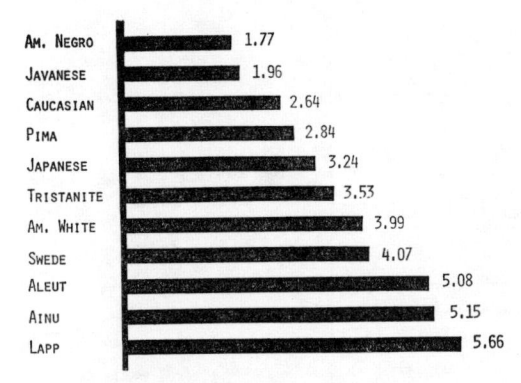

Population	Value
Am. Negro	1.77
Javanese	1.96
Caucasian	2.64
Pima	2.84
Japanese	3.24
Tristanite	3.53
Am. White	3.99
Swede	4.07
Aleut	5.08
Ainu	5.15
Lapp	5.66

Figure 2. Mahalanobis' Generalized Distance between Aborigines and Other Populations (Permanent, Males)

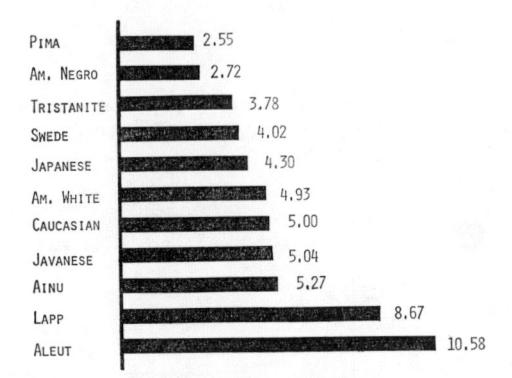

Population	Value
Pima	2.55
Am. Negro	2.72
Tristanite	3.78
Swede	4.02
Japanese	4.30
Am. White	4.93
Caucasian	5.00
Javanese	5.04
Ainu	5.27
Lapp	8.67
Aleut	10.58

Figure 3. Mahalanobis' Generalized Distance between Aborigines and Other Populations (Permanent, Females)

tions in the male and female groups, respectively. Although there are some discrepancies in the order of populations, being arranged in increasing order of distances, between males and females, they share some other characteristics in common. The remarkable point is that the distance between Aborigines and American Negroes is very small both in males and females. Similar to this, Pimas are the closest to Aborigines in females, and relatively close in males. This might be caused by relatively large size of the teeth in the three populations. Another remarkable point is that the Caucasian populations which represent the smallest teeth are not necessarily most far from Aborigines. This seems to be related to more or less extent of similarities in the relative size of teeth, or tooth groups, among these populations. Further, it is of quite interest to note that Aborigines are most far from the northern people such as Aleuts, Ainu and Norwegian Lapps. The results appear to show dissimilarities in relative tooth size rather than in absolute size of teeth.

In order to recognize relative locations of each population which is scattered in a multi-dimensional space, two-dimensional scattergrams were drawn on the basis of the first and second canonical variates which were computed by Rao's method (1952). Figures 4 and 5 are scattergrams for males and females, respectively.

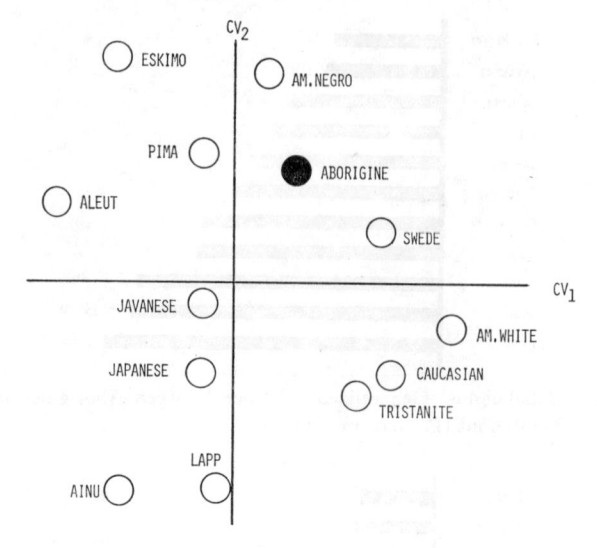

Figure 4. Two-Dimensional Expression of Group Constellation Based on the First and Second Canonical Variates I and II (Permanent, Males)

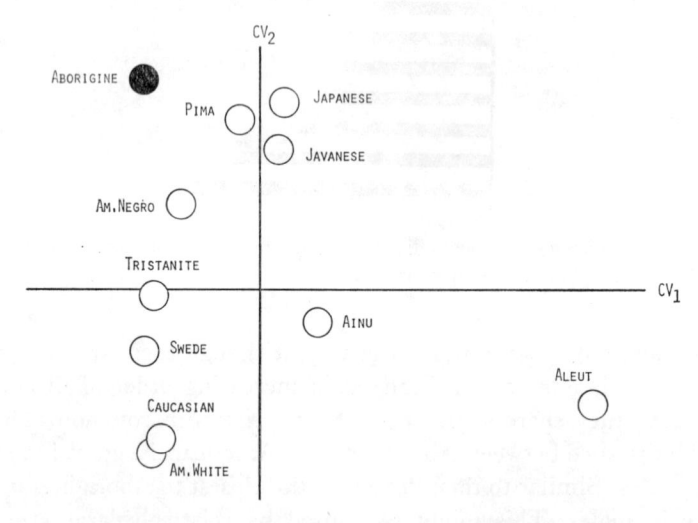

Figure 5. Two-Dimensional Expression of Group Constellations Based on the Canonical Variates I and II (Permanent, Females)

In Figure 4 clustering is hardly possible since each population is scattered separately. However, if we pay attention to the first canonical variates (CV_1 axis), it is evident that the populations presented here might be grouped into four clusters—Aleut-Ainu cluster, Pima-Javanese-Japanese-Lapp cluster, American Negro-Aborigine cluster, and Swede-Caucasian-Tristanite-American White cluster.

In the same manner, females (Figure 5) could be grouped into three clusters—Aborigine-American Negro-Tristanite-Swede-Caucasian-American White cluster, Pima-Japanese-Javanese-Ainu cluster, and Aleut cluster.

In both cases, Aborigines are located closer to American Negroes and Pimas and far from the northern peoples. Japanese and Caucasian populations are intermediate in distance from Aborigines.

4.5.2. Penrose's Shape Distance Based on the Mesiodistal Crown Diameters of the Permanent and Deciduous Dentitions

There has been some criticism of similarity coefficients which represent the so-called biological distance. For instance, Corruccini (1973) stated that "only size differences were detected by the C.R.L., Penrose's size distance, D^2, and canonical variates, and as a result these methods failed to produce an accurate classification," and further goes to state that "Penrose's shape distance and Q-mode correlation coefficients produced better results due to their determination of similarity on the basis of more important shape and morphological differences."

Although there might be some argument against such a recognition, it is of great importance to compare populations in terms of shape component. Sokal and Sneath (1963) strongly recommended the use of Q-mode correlation coefficients to obtain taxonomically more important informations, but the author employed Penrose's shape distance simply because the computer program was easily available.

Figures 6 and 7 illustrate shape distance between Aborigines and other populations on the basis of mesiodistal crown diameters in the male and female permanent dentitions, respectively. The pooled standard deviations were calculated from standard deviations given for each population.

It is quite evident from Figure 6 that, in the male permanent dentition, Aborigines are most close to Caucasian populations and most far from the northern populations such as Aleuts, Lapps and Ainu; and Javanese, Japanese and American Negroes being in between. It is of interest to note that the large difference between Aborigines and northern populations is recognized in generalized distance and shape distance in common (see Figure 2). In contrast to this, Caucasian populations which are located relatively far from Aborigines in generalized distance come close to the latter in shape distance.

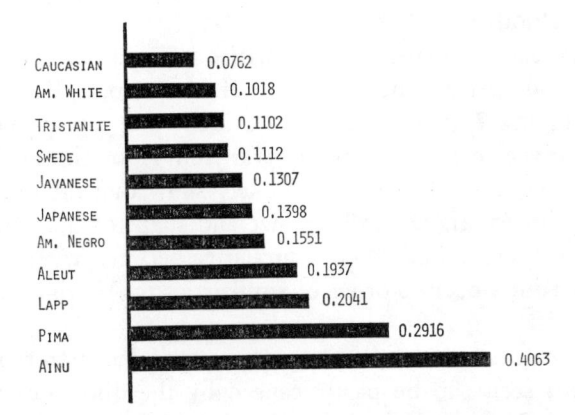

Population	Value
Caucasian	0.0762
Am. White	0.1018
Tristanite	0.1102
Swede	0.1112
Javanese	0.1307
Japanese	0.1398
Am. Negro	0.1551
Aleut	0.1937
Lapp	0.2041
Pima	0.2916
Ainu	0.4063

Figure 6. Penrose's Shape Distance between Aborigines and Other Populations (Permanent, Males)

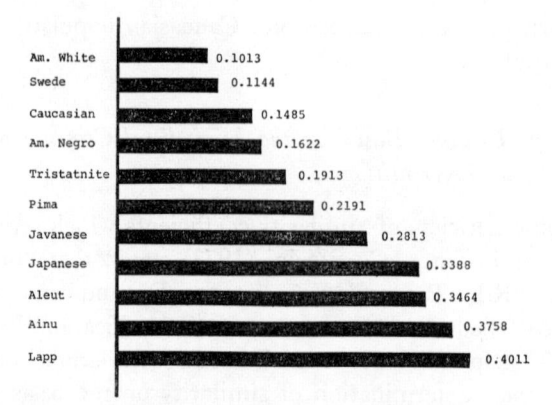

Population	Distance
Am. White	0.1013
Swede	0.1144
Caucasian	0.1485
Am. Negro	0.1622
Tristatnite	0.1913
Pima	0.2191
Javanese	0.2813
Japanese	0.3388
Aleut	0.3464
Ainu	0.3758
Lapp	0.4011

Figure 7. Penrose's Shape Distance between Aborigines and Other Populations (Permanent, Females)

Almost the same trends can be seen in the female permanent dentition in more typical fashion than in the male dentition. In Figure 7, at least four groups may be classified by the order from the smallest to the largest shape distance: American White-Swede-Caucasian group, American Negro-Tristanite group, Pima-Javanese-Japanese group, and Aleut-Ainu-Lapp group. This trend seems to be quite suggestive for analysis of population affinity of the Aboriginal dentition.

As to the comparison between Mahalanobis' generalized distance and Penrose's shape distance, there is naturally a certain extent of difference caused by the difference between the two methods. There are, however, some common features in the results obtained by both methods.

In order to recognize overall relationship between the two kinds of distances, correlation coefficients were calculated from the distance coefficients for the male and female permanent dentitions (see Figures 2–3 and 6–7). Correlation coefficients for males, 0.40 with 9 degrees of freedom, and those for females, 0.59 with 9 degrees of freedom, are both insignificant under the 5% level. These results show that the overall relationships between the two sets of distance coefficients under consideration can be regarded as independent of each other.

There are, nevertheless, remarkable similarities between the two sets of distances both in male and female permanent dentitions. If we compare Figure 2 with Figure 6 and Figure 3 with Figure 7, it becomes quite evident that the northern populations—Aleuts, Ainu and Norwegian Lapps—are most far from Aborigines either in generalized distance or in shape distance. These results likely show that the northern populations are quite different from Aborigines in both size and shape of the permanent dentition. In regard to the other populations, such a similarity between the two sets of distances can be hardly pointed out since the order of similarities to Aborigines varies to a larger extent.

In contrast to the permanent dentition, the deciduous dentition represents somewhat different trends. This seems to be partly caused by the difference in the number of populations compared. Nevertheless, the order of similarities to Aborigines are largely different from that of the permanent dentition. In Figures 8 and 9, it is commonly seen

4. Tooth Crown Measurements

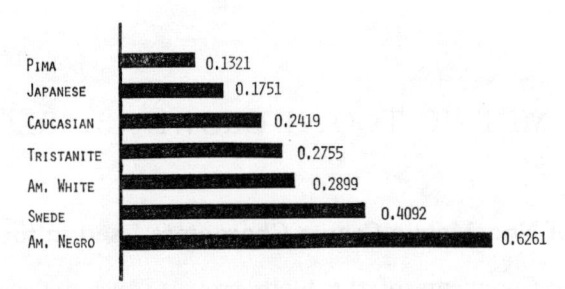

Population	Value
Pima	0.1321
Japanese	0.1751
Caucasian	0.2419
Tristanite	0.2755
Am. White	0.2899
Swede	0.4092
Am. Negro	0.6261

Figure 8. Penrose's Shape Distance between Aborigines and Other Populations (Deciduous, Males)

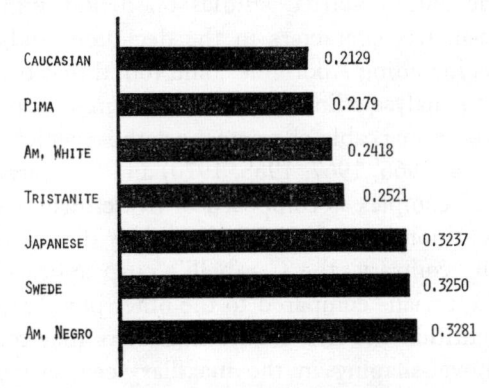

Population	Value
Caucasian	0.2129
Pima	0.2179
Am. White	0.2418
Tristanite	0.2521
Japanese	0.3237
Swede	0.3250
Am. Negro	0.3281

Figure 9. Penrose's Shape Distance between Aborigines and Other Populations (Deciduous, Females)

that the Mongoloid populations are the closest to Aborigines, and Swedes and American Negroes are farthest from the latter.

In his factor analysis study of the deciduous dentition, Hanihara (1974) characterized Aboriginal and Japanese deciduous dentitions as 'molar type' in which the back teeth were comparatively larger, and Caucasians and Pimas as 'incisor type' where the front teeth were relatively larger. According to the same author (1976), on the other hand, the permanent dentition of Aborigines and Caucasians is 'molar type' and that of Japanese is 'incisor-canine type'.

These results apparently show that the 'shape' of the teeth probably differs between the deciduous and permanent dentitions even in the same population. The discrepancies in shape distance between both dentitions may stem from difference in shape component between the two dentitions. At all events, the shape distance of the deciduous dentition shows that Pimas and Caucasians are relatively close to Aborigines, Swedes and American Negroes far from the latter, and the order of similarity of the remaining populations varies between males and females.

5. NON-METRIC TOOTH CROWN CHARACTERS

5.1. Description of Non-Metric Crown Characters Used in the Present Study

In addition to measurements of the tooth crowns, several non-metric characters which appeared on the crowns may provide important informations in regard to taxonomic problems of human populations.

Since 1954 when the author started studies on dental anthropology, he has accumulated data on non-metric characters in the deciduous and permanent dentitions from several populations including Aborigines, and found that their frequency distributions were quite useful to analyse affinities between different populations.

Among these, the most remarkable characters are those which are called 'Mongoloid dental complex' (Hanihara, 1966, 1967, 1968, 1970) and the Carabelli's cusp.

The Mongoloid dental complex is composed of five crown characters which characterize the Mongoloid dentition in their higher frequency distributions than in the other populations, and, on the contrary, the Carabelli's cusp appears more frequently and predominantly in the Caucasians compared to the other populations.

In the permanent dentition the five crown characters that compose the Mongoloid dental complex are: shovel-shaping in the maxillary central incisors, cusp 6, cusp 7, deflecting wrinkle and protostylid in the mandibular first molars; while in the deciduous dentition they are the same characters in the deciduous maxillary incisors and the deciduous mandibular second molars. In the deciduous dentition, frequency of the Carabelli's cusp was calculated from those in the deciduous maxillary second molars.

There is another problem in observing non-metric characters in regard to criteria for classification. In the present study the teeth which carry the corresponding characters were distinguished from non-carriers in the following manner:

1) *Shovel shape*—This character has so far been classified into some categories such as no-shovel, slight-shovel, moderate-shovel, etc., through non-metric observations. However, the most ideal way to measure the extent of shovelling might be to make a direct measurement of depth of the lingual fossa in the incisors.

For this purpose, as already described in Section 4.1.3 of this paper, the author used a dial gauge with a pair of movable arms to measure the extent of shovelling in the maxillary central incisors. In the present study, the teeth with the lingual fossa which equals to or less than 0.5 mm depth were classified into 'no-shovel', and those which are deeper than 0.5 mm into carriers of the shovel trait.

On the other hand, since the depth of the lingual fossa is generally much smaller in the deciduous maxillary central incisors than in the permanent incisors, no direct measurement was made for them. Instead of this, each tooth was compared to the Plaque D1 which was prepared to classify the shovelling in the deciduous maxillary central incisors (Hanihara, 1961). This plaque illustrates four developmental stages of the shovel traits by attaching figures 0 through 3: 0 for no-shovel, 1 for trace- or semi-shovel, 2 for moderate-shovel, and 3 for strong-shovel. In the present study, the teeth classified into stages 0 and 1 were combined and referred to as 'no-shovel', and those classified into stages 2 and 3 were joined together to make another category of 'shovel'.

The reason for such a simplification is based on the fact that the former group of teeth may, through genetic analysis of the Japanese-American F_1 hybrids, be regarded as non-carriers and the latter groups as carriers of this trait (Hanihara, 1965). The morphological differences between stages 0 and 1 as well as between 2 and 3 may thus be considered to be accidental variations caused by non-genetic factors.

2) *Cusp 6*—This cusp is one of the extra cusps which appears occasionally between the entoconid and hypoconulid in the permanent and deciduous mandibular molars. The incidence of this cusp has been studied by several investigators and regarded as a racial characteristic (Hellman, 1928; Dahlberg, 1945; Tratman, 1950; Suzuki and Sakai, 1956; Hanihara, 1966, 1968; etc.). Distinction of carriers and non-carriers of this trait is quite easy, so that the teeth with this cusp were simply counted as carriers regardless of size.

3) *Cusp 7*—This is another extra cusp which is located at the marginal border between the metaconid and the entoconid. This cusp was originally described by Selenka (1898) who proposed the term *tuberculum accessorium mediale internum*, and reported many incidences by several subsequent authors in the fossil and recent primates including man. For instance, de Terra (1905) reported frequencies of this cusp in the permanent mandibular molars of recent man, and Suzuki and Sakai (1956) made a statistical investigation in Japanese. On the other hand, the cusp in the deciduous mandibular molars was reported by Robinson (1958), Jørgensen (1956), Hanihara and Minamidate (1965), Hanihara (1966, 1967, 1970), etc.

In the permanent mandibular first molars, the cusp 7 appears in relatively rare cases, but its expression is quite evident. According to Suzuki and Sakai (1965), the cusp 7 appears to be stemming from the metaconid in most of the cases, but rarely it may be regarded as branching from the entoconid. In the present study, both cases were counted as carriers of this trait in the permanent mandibular first molars.

On the other hand, the cusp 7 appears to vary its expressivity continuously in the deciduous mandibular second molars. On the basis of this fact, the Plaque D9 (see Hanihara, 1961) illustrates four stages of this cusp which were arranged in a serial order from absent (stage 0), through trace (stage 1) and medium (stage 2), to well-developed (stage 3). In this study, as in the case of the shovelling in the deciduous maxillary central incisors, each tooth was classified into the corresponding stages by comparing to the Plaque D9 to warrant objectivity of the classification, and the teeth classified either into stages 1, 2 or 3 were referred to as carriers of this trait.

4) *Deflecting wrinkle*—The deflecting wrinkle is one of the particular formations of the median ridge of the metaconid. The ridge, when the deflecting wrinkle appears, shows a stronger development in either its length or breadth and curves distalward at the central part of the occlusal surface.

This character was first described by Weidenreich (1937, 1945) in his papers on *Sinanthropus* and *Gigantopithecus*, and subsequently, von Koenigswald (1952) drew attention to the deflecting wrinkle appeared in the deciduous mandibular molars in modern Javanese. In addition, the frequency distribution of this character in Japanese permanent molars was reported by Suzuki and Sakai (1956) and those in Japanese permanent and deciduous molars by Hanihara et al. (1964) and Hanihara (1970).

According to Hanihara, Kuwashima and Sakao (1964), there are considerably wide range of varieties in appearance of the deflecting wrinkle. For instance, in some cases, the wrinkle is of relatively simple form in which the median ridge of the metaconid is well-developed but deflected little, whereas in the other cases, the ridge is typically deflected at almost a right angle.

In the present study, only the teeth with the wrinkles which deflected at about a right angle were referred to as carriers of this trait, and those showing little deflection were disregarded even if the median ridge was well-developed. This rule was applied to permanent and deciduous mandibular molars in common.

5) *Protostylid*—The term protostylid was first proposed by Dahlberg (1945, 1949, 1950) for a swelling or an extra cusp found on the buccal surface of the protoconid in the mandibular molars.

The original author reported extremely high frequencies of this character in Pima Indians in comparison with the other populations in which it is only rarely observed. Later, Suzuki and Sakai (1954) found fairly frequent appearance of the protostylid in the mandibular molars of Japanese. These findings proved that the protostylid occurred very rarely in the dentition of modern man with the exception of some particular populations such as mentioned above.

In his studies of the deciduous dentition, Hanihara (1956, 1966) reported that the protostylid was relatively frequently observed in the deciduous mandibular second molars, though it showed generally less degree of prominence compared with the permanent molars. The same author (1968) also reported frequencies of this extra cusp in some different populations, and found significant difference between Mongoloids and other populations.

Although there are many varieties in expression of the protostylid, the author counted, in the present study, only those teeth which showed a more or less extent of swelling on the buccal surface as carriers of this trait, the so-called pit or furrow type having been omitted from calculation of frequencies.

6) *Carabelli's cusp*—It is well known that the Carabelli's cusp frequently appears in Caucasoids and relatively infrequently in non-Caucasoid populations. At the same time, the cusp is generally well developed in the former populations. In this connection, this cusp is not included in the Mongoloid dental complex described above, but it rather characterizes Caucasoid populations in its higher frequencies.

There are again several varieties in its appearance illustrated by Dahlberg's Plaque P12 for permanent dentition and by Hanihara's Plaque D7 for deciduous dentition (Hanihara, 1961). In the present study, however, those forms which are separated from the lingual surface by a groove and, as a result, possess a more or less free apex were counted for statistical procedures. Such a method of classification may provide a reasonal basis to distinguish the Caucasoids from the other populations.

5.2. Frequencies of Non-Metric Crown Characters in the Permanent Dentition

Table 28 gives percentile frequencies of each crown character in the seven popula-

Table 28. Frequencies of Non-Metric Crown Characters in Permanent Dentitions (in %, Males and Females Combined)

Population	Shovel-shape (I^1)	Cusp 6 (M_1)	Cusp 7 (M_1)	Defl. Wrinkle (M_1)	Protostylid (M_1)	Carabelli's Cusp (M^1)
Aborigine	89.8 (166)	52.5 (162)	6.5 (155)	41.1 (163)	6.1 (165)	15.7 (159)
Japanese	95.6 (432)	25.3 (1046)	6.7 (50)	29.6 (395)	6.6 (425)	6.5 (444)
Ainu	81.4 (97)	26.6 (79)	4.8 (83)	25.6 (78)	12.2 (82)	9.5 (105)
Pima	99.1 (222)	26.6 (207)	8.2 (208)	39.5 (205)	19.4 (217)	6.9 (216)
Eskimo	100.0 (21)	50.0 (30)	20.0 (30)	44.4 (27)	28.6 (14)	13.0 (23)
Caucasian	27.7 (83)	5.2 (58)	5.1 (59)	3.6 (56)	0.0 (81)	39.0 (59)
Am. Negro	37.2 (78)	6.5 (77)	43.6 (78)	16.3 (80)	0.0 (78)	16.3 (80)

Figures in parentheses show the sample numbers.

tions on which observations were made by the present author. Although there are a number of similar data reported by previous authors, comparison was carried out only for the above populations because criteria for classifying characters might have been more or less different one another. The data shown here are those from males and females in combination since no between-sex difference was observed.

For the shovel-shaped character in the maxillary central incisors, there is a distinct difference between the Caucasian-American Negro group and the rest of the populations. In particular, considerably high frequencies are shown by Japanese, Pimas and Eskimos, and a little less frequencies by Aborigines and Ainu.

Frequencies of the cusp 6 show again a distinct contrast between the former and the latter groups of populations. In this character, however, Aborigines represent the highest frequency which is followed by Eskimos, and it is of interest to note that Japanese, Ainu and Pimas show almost the same frequencies.

In regard to the cusp 7, American Negroes show the highest frequency which is largely different from those of the other populations. As described later, difference in frequencies of this character is much greater in the deciduous molars.

The deflecting wrinkle appears quite frequently in Aborigines, Pimas and Eskimos, a little less in Japanese and Ainu, and relatively rarely in Caucasians and American Negroes.

Frequencies of the protostylid are the highest in Eskimos followed by Pimas, and relatively low in Aborigines, Japanese and Ainu. In Caucasians and American Negroes practically no incidence of this character was observed.

As already mentioned above, the Carabelli's cusp shows different trends from the other characters just described. The incidence of this character is the highest in Caucasians and much less in the other populations. Among the latter, however, Aborigines and American Negroes show relatively high frequencies of the Carabelli's cusp in comparison with Japanese, Ainu and Pimas, Eskimos being located in between.

As a whole, Aborigines are similar to the Mongoloid populations in frequency distribution of the crown characters which compose the Mongoloid dental complex. In the Carabelli's cusp, however, the frequency in Aborigines is almost equal to that of American Negroes and intermediate between those of the Mongoloids and Caucasians.

5.3. Frequencies of Non-Metric Crown Characters in the Deciduous Dentition

Table 29 gives percentile frequencies of non-metric crown characters in the deciduous dentition. As in the permanent dentition already described, the populations observed by the present author were compared.

For the shovel-shaping character in the deciduous maxillary central incisors, there is a clear-cut difference between the upper five populations in Table 29 and the lower two populations, in spite of small numbers of samples in some populations. This trend is quite similar to that of the permanent dentition.

Almost the same results are obtained from the data for the cusp 6. It is remarkable that frequency in Aborigines is much higher than in the other populations. The same result is also reported by Kuusk (1973) who obtained frequency of 65.0% out of 177 deciduous mandibular second molars in Aborigines.

The deflecting wrinkle is also as frequent in Aborigines as in the Mongoloid populations. The frequencies are almost equal in these populations but much less in Caucasians and American Negroes.

The protostylid is most frequently observed in Pimas as reported by Dahlberg (1949), and a little less in Eskimos. Aborigines show a similar frequency to Japanese and Ainu, and Caucasians and American Negroes show less frequencies.

As in the permanent maxillary first molars, the incidence of the Carabelli's cusp is the highest in Caucasians and a little less in Aborigines. Japanese, Ainu and American Negroes show nearly equal frequencies and the cusp is practically absent in Pimas and Eskimos.

In general, trends observed in the deciduous dentition are quite parallel to those of the permanent dentition with a small discrepancy between them. To evaluate such similarities, correlation coefficients were calculated on the basis of frequencies in the deciduous and permanent dentitions. The coefficients are 0.91 for shovel-shaping, 0.88 for cusp 6, −0.31 for cusp 7, 0.88 for deflecting wrinkle, 0.86 for protostylid, and 0.81 for Carabelli's cusp. Of these only the correlation coefficient for the cusp 7 is insignificant and the rest of the coefficients are significant under the 5% level. The result in the cusp 7 is very likely caused by a remarkably higher frequency in American Negro permanent molars.

Table 29. Frequencies of Non-Metric Crown Characters in Deciduous Dentition (in %, Males and Females Combined)

Population	Shovel-shape (di^1)	Cusp 6 (dm_2)	Cusp 7 (dm_2)	Defl. Wrinkle (dm_2)	Protostylid (dm_2)	Carabell's Cusp (dm^2)
Aborigine	76.3 (38)	68.1 (72)	63.3 (90)	74.6 (71)	36.8 (76)	21.0 (105)
Japanese	76.6 (124)	36.9 (92)	73.7 (156)	71.6 (201)	44.7 (152)	11.9 (185)
Ainu	50.0 (4)	23.8 (21)	71.4 (21)	70.0 (20)	45.5 (22)	16.0 (25)
Pima	61.6 (78)	36.8 (117)	72.9 (118)	84.3 (115)	89.0 (118)	0.0 (118)
Eskimo	50.0 (16)	37.7 (33)	79.4 (63)	67.9 (53)	67.3 (52)	0.0 (66)
Caucasian	0.0 (20)	7.3 (55)	40.7 (54)	13.0 (54)	14.5 (55)	35.7 (56)
Am. Negro	20.0 (10)	12.0 (50)	46.8 (47)	19.1 (47)	19.1 (47)	11.8 (51)

Figures in parentheses show the sample numbers.

Comparison of Tables 28 and 29 shows that the difference in frequencies between Mongoloids and other populations are much more remarkable in the deciduous dentition than in the permanent dentition. From this fact it may be assumed that the deciduous dentition preserves generalized characters to a larger extent than the permanent dentition, and the latter provides more informations in regard to specificity of each population than the former.

In this respect, Aborigines seem to be closer to Mongoloids than to Caucasians and American Negroes. However, there are some characters whose frequencies are predominantly high in Aborigines and, in the other characters, they are intermediate between both extreme cases. In this connection, it is quite difficult to postulate general affinity of Aborigines from direct comparison of frequencies of each character involved.

5.4. Affinities of Populations Viewed from Biological Distance Based on the Non-Metric Crown Characters

A considerable number of methods which determine the biological distance based on non-metric characters, or qualitative variables, have so far been proposed. Among these, the most suitable methods for the present study may be those devised by R. A. Fisher and C. A. B. Smith (Berry and Berry, 1967; Constandse-Westermann, 1972). In particular, Smith's method has some advantages over Fisher's method in providing more evident difference between populations and ease of test of significance.

According to Berry and Berry (1967), the distance will be significant at the 0.05 probability level if it is greater than three times of variance, and at the 0.01 level if it is greater than six times of variance.

The original equations for calculating distance coefficient (D) and its variance (V) given by Smith are:

$$D = [\sum_{i=1}^{N}(\theta_{Ii}-\theta_{IIi})^2/N] - (1/n_{Ii}+1/n_{IIi}) \qquad (1)$$

and

$$V = [4(1/n_I+1/n_{II})\sum_{i=1}^{N}(\theta_{Ii}-\theta_{IIi})^2/N] - 4(1/n_I+1/n_{II}) \qquad (2)$$

where $\theta_{Ii} = \sin^{-1}(1-2p_{Ii})$, p_{Ii} is frequency for i-th character in population I, and N stands for the number of characters involved.

However, these forms do not allow the use of sample numbers which differ for each trait under consideration. To obtain distance coefficients and their variances based on different sample numbers the above formulae should be modified as follows (Hanihara et al., 1974):

$$D = \sum_{i=1}^{N}[(\theta_{Ii}-\theta_{IIi})^2 - (1/n_{Ii}+1/n_{IIi})]/N \qquad (3)$$

and

$$V = \sum_{i=1}^{N}[4(1/n_{Ii}+1/n_{IIi})\{(\theta_{Ii}-\theta_{IIi})^2 - (1/n_{Ii}+1/n_{IIi})\}]/N. \qquad (4)$$

In Tables 30 and 31 distances and variances computed by the equations (3) and (4) for permanent and deciduous dentitions are shown. Every distance coefficient is larger

Table 30. Smith's Distance between Populations Based on Non-Metric Crown Characters in Permanent Dentition

Population	Aborigine	Japanese	Ainu	Pima	Eskimo	Caucasian	Am. Negro
Aborigine	—						
Japanese	.0762 .0021	—					
Ainu	.0727 .0054	.0315 .0014	—				
Pima	.1152 .0050	.0335 .0008	.0919 .0056	—			
Eskimo	.1163 .0296	.1384 .0295	.2125 .0472	.0330 .0040	—		
Caucasian	.7813 .0660	.7310 .0470	.5035 .0512	1.0226 0.753	1.3394 .3272	—	
Am. Negro	.6537 .0497	.5803 .0427	.4436 .0433	.8083 .0565	1.0100 .2486	.2198 .0262	—

Upper rows show distances and lower rows variances.

Table 31. Smith's Distance between Populations Based on Non-Metric Crown Characters in Deciduous Dentition

Population	Aborigine	Japanese	Ainu	Pima	Eskimo	Caucasian	Am. Negro
Aborigine	—						
Japanese	.0693 .0062	—					
Ainu	.1128 .0324	.0180 .0041	—				
Pima	.4537 .0380	.2672 .0159	.2277 .0180	—			
Eskimo	.3137 .0466	.1404 .0197	.0600 .0041	.0510 .0048	—		
Caucasian	1.4388 .3155	1.3061 .2289	.7853 .5464	1.8457 .2745	1.3024 .3109	—	
Am. Negro	.7319 .1810	.5710 .1348	.2653 .0867	1.0181 .1571	.5839 .1142	.1558 .0765	—

Upper rows show distances and lower rows variances.

than three times of variance so that all of them are significant under the 5% level, or even under the 1% level in some cases.

It is quite evident that Aborigines show a very close affinity to the Mongoloid populations in both permanent and deciduous dentitions, but are very far from Caucasians and American Negroes. These results are quite different from those of the crown measurements described in the previous chapter. It is no wonder, however, that the results from the metric and non-metric characters are different each other. Existence and non-existence of certain crown characters, the cusp 6 in the deciduous mandibular second molars, for example, show practically no correlation with the mesiodistal crown diameters of the same teeth ($r=0.25$, $DF=58$; Hanihara, unpublished data).

On the other hand, Smith's distances in the deciduous and permanent dentitions

5. Non-Metric Tooth Crown Characters 45

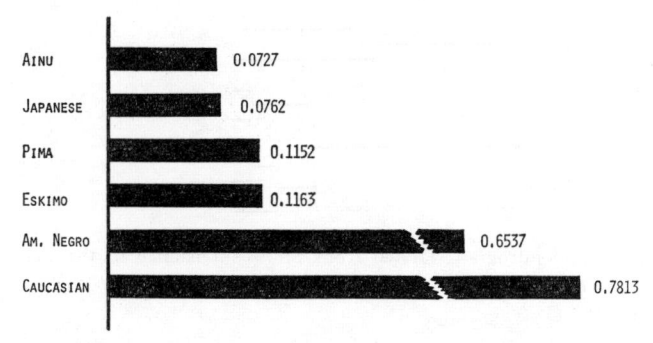

Ainu	0.0727
Japanese	0.0762
Pima	0.1152
Eskimo	0.1163
Am. Negro	0.6537
Caucasian	0.7813

Figure 10. Smith's Distance between Aborigines and Other Populations (Permanent)

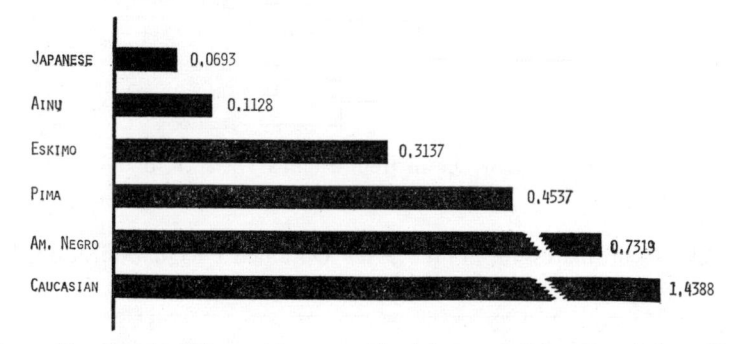

Japanese	0.0693
Ainu	0.1128
Eskimo	0.3137
Pima	0.4537
Am. Negro	0.7319
Caucasian	1.4388

Figure 11. Smith's Distance between Aborigines and Other Populations (Deciduous)

show quite similar trends each other. Correlation coefficient between distances for both dentitions is 0.85 ($DF=19$) and this is highly significant at the 0.01 probability level (Figures 10 and 11). This shows clearly that frequencies of the crown characters involved vary quite similarly in the permanent and deciduous dentitions within the same population.

From the distances shown in Tables 30 and 31, clustering of populations is not necessarily easy because each population is scattered in a six-dimensional space. However, affinities between populations may be roughly expressed by a dendrogram if minor contradictions can be disregarded.

For the permanent dentition, a dendrogram like that shown in Figure 12 may be drawn using a usual technique of clustering. In the same manner, another dendrogram for the deciduous dentition can be drawn as shown in Figure 13. Both dendrograms are almost the same in shape, and this is quite natural because the distance coefficients are, as mentioned above, quite similar to each other in the permanent and deciduous dentitions.

For clustering populations, another statistical technique may be employed. Since the distances calculated are those in a multi-dimensional space, relative location of each population may be hardly comprehensive. To reduce such difficulties, statistical treatment based on model IV of quantification theory was employed. This model has been proposed by Hayashi (1952, 1954) to express affinities among several catagories, or populations in the present case, in a space of reduced dimensions.

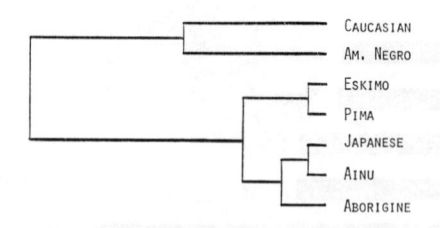

Figure 12. A Dendrogram Drawn from Smith's Distance in the Permanent Dentition

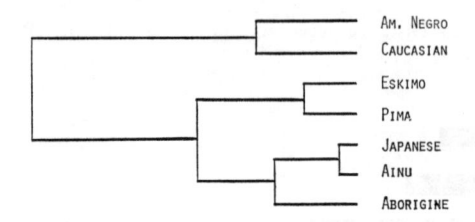

Figure 13. A Dendrogram Drawn from Smith's Distance in the Deciduous Dentition

Table 32. Coordinates for Three Axes Obtained by Quantification Theory Model IV (Permanent Dentition)

Population	Z_1	Z_2	Z_3
Aborigine	0.6114	0.1384	−1.7001
Japanese	0.6017	0.1125	−0.5804
Ainu	0.5916	0.1036	−0.3883
Pima	0.6447	0.1266	1.7102
Eskimo	0.6802	0.1418	0.8179
Caucasian	−1.9148	1.5226	−0.0255
Am. Negro	−1.1848	−2.1454	0.1662

Table 33. Coordinates for Three Axes Obtained by Quantification Theory Model IV (Deciduous Dentition)

Population	Z_1	Z_2	Z_3
Aborigine	0.6234	0.0605	−1.4737
Japanese	0.5717	0.0924	−0.3234
Ainu	0.5401	0.0706	−0.8848
Pima	0.7148	0.2540	0.7564
Eskimo	0.6357	0.1795	1.8342
Caucasian	−1.9408	1.4977	0.0476
Am. Negro	−1.1449	−2.1547	0.0437

In the present study, reciprocals of Smith's distances were used as parameters which represent affinities between populations. The final scores are shown in Tables 32 and 33, and Figures 14 and 15 were drawn by using the first two scores (Z_1 and Z_2) as co-

5. Non-Metric Tooth Crown Characters

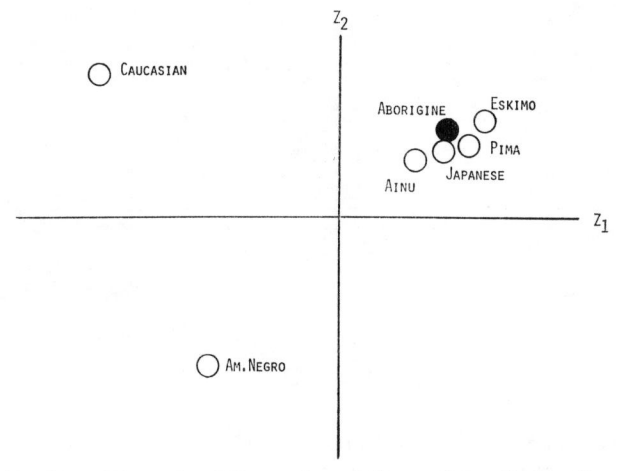

Figure 14. Two-Dimensional Expression of Group Constellations Based on Z_1 and Z_2 Scores (Permanent)

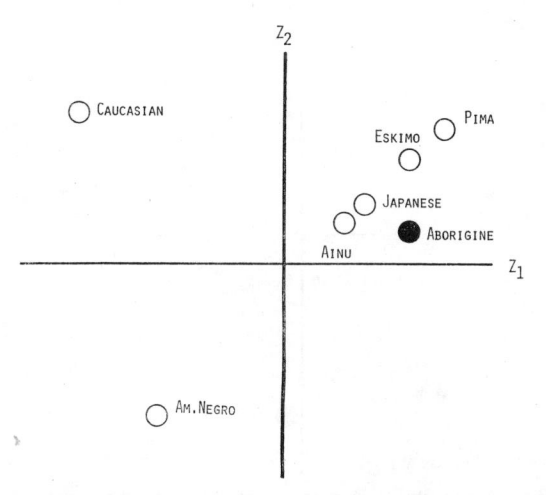

Figure 15. Two-Dimensional Expression of Group Constellations Based on Z_1 and Z_2 Scores (Deciduous)

ordinates for each population. Geometrically speaking, this procedure means that, in the present case, the populations scattered in a six-dimensional space are projected to a two-dimensional space with a minimum loss of informations.

It may be easily assumed from Tables 32 and 33 that, in both deciduous and permanent dentitions, Caucasians and American Negroes occupy quite different locations from each other and from the rest of the populations. On the other hand, the latter five populations are located very close to each other as they would represent a single cluster. This is clearly shown in Figures 14 and 15.

However, it is of interest to note that clustering may become quite easy if we pay attention to the third scores (Z_3). The Z_3-values for the first five populations seem to distinguish the following three clusters: Aborigines, Japanese-Ainu, and Pima-Eskimo clusters (Figures 16 and 17).

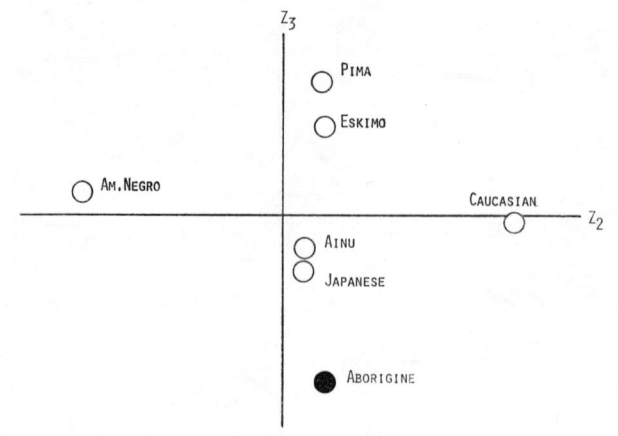

Figure 16. Two-Dimensional Expression of Group Constellations Based on Z_2 and Z_3 Scores (Permanent)

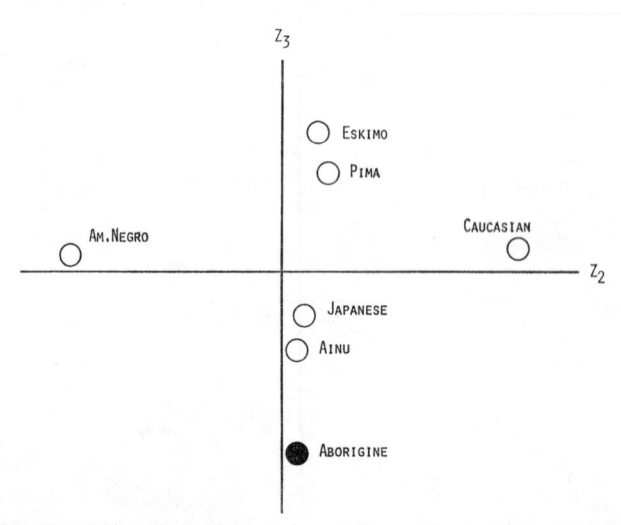

Figure 17. Two-Dimensional Expression of Group Constellation Based on Z_2 and Z_3 Scores (Deciduous)

From what we mentioned above, it may be concluded that 1) Caucasians and American Negroes are apparently separated from each other as well as from the rest of the populations involved, so that each of the former two populations may be supposed to compose different clusters, and 2) Aborigines, Japanese, Ainu, Pimas and Eskimos are very closely located, but if we pay an attention to the Z_3-scores, it becomes evident that three clusters can be distinguished: Aborigine cluster, Japanese-Ainu cluster, and Pima-Eskimo cluster.

These results are quite agreeable with Figures 12 and 13 which were drawn by rather elementary clustering techniques. At the same time, it may be noteworthy that the clusters thus established agree with geographical relationship of populations involved, although the Aborigine cluster is very close to those of Mongoloids in terms of biological distance.

6. DISCUSSION

In this chapter, affinities of Aborigines viewed from dental characteristics will be discussed. As already mentioned, an extent of affinity of this population is different from character to character so that it is rather difficult to find a uniform conclusion which is compatible with all or most of the data presented in this paper.

Comparison of the mesiodistal crown diameters shows that Aborigines appear to represent the largest teeth among the populations compared in the present study. However, Pimas have also large teeth which are almost comparable with or, in some teeth, even exceed those of Aborigines. In this connection, it can hardly be concluded that the Aboriginal dentition is extraordinarily larger than that in any other modern populations. But it is still true that the former is much larger than the dentition in Caucasians and most of the Mongoloid populations. Difference between Aborigines and American Negroes is relatively small.

Shovel trait is most remarkable in Mongoloid populations, intermediate in Aborigines and much less in Caucasians and American Negroes. This likely shows that Aborigines are largely different from both Mongoloids and Caucasian-American Negro group in regard to this character.

Mahalanobis' generalized distances show that Aborigines are relatively close to Pimas and American Negroes, and far from the northern populations such as Ainu, Aleuts and Norwegian Lapps, Japanese and Caucasians being in between. The results seem to stress that Aborigines show less affinity to the northern people. In addition, a close affinity between Aborigines and Pimas as well as American Negroes is probably related to similarity in overall tooth size among these populations.

Quite interestingly, Penrose's shape distances show a close affinity between Aborigines and Caucasians, and again much less affinity between the former and the northern populations. If a view stressed by several previous authors that the shape component is much more important in the taxonomic problems can be adopted, special attention should be paid to the results obtained from the shape distance. In this regard, the following opinion expressed by Abbie (1969) might be of special importance: "It is quite logical, on our present knowledge at least, to class the Aborigines as proto-Caucasoids" (p. 219). A close affinity between Aborigines and Caucasians is also proved by the similarity in pattern of between-sex difference described in Section 4.2 of the present paper.

As to the frequency distributions of some non-metric characters, Aborigines are very close to the Mongoloids and far from Caucasians and American Negroes as shown by the Smith's distance coefficients. It should be noted that most of the non-metric characters compared are those considered to be of archaic origin in the course of human evolution, with only exception of the Carabelli's cusp. In this connection, Aborigines seem to share the archaic dental characters in common with the Mongoloids to a considerably large extent.

As mentioned above, the affinities of dental traits in Aborigines can hardly be concluded in a simple form, because they are largely different from character to character. However, perhaps one fact which may be safely concluded is that Aborigines show a larger extent of archaic dental characters in almost every respect of the present study. At the same time, it should be also pointed out that the extent of retention of archaic dental characters in Aborigines might not be so largely different from those of some other populations such as Eskimos and Pimas.

In addition, it seems to be of great importance that Aborigines are largely different from the northern populations in either Mahalanobis' distance or Penrose's shape distance. This evidently proves that these populations are different from each other in absolute size as well as in size proportions of the dentition.

Finally, the relationship between Aborigines and Ainu should be mentioned here on the basis of the results obtained from the dental characters. A close affinity between the two populations has been stressed since de Saint-Martin (1872) and later authors such as Anutschin (1876–1907), Debetz (1947, 1951), Levin (1958), etc. (see Kodama, 1970).

On the contrary, Yamaguchi (1967) and Omoto (1972) opposed this view based on the skeletal characteristics and biochemical polymorphisms of enzymes and proteins. Further, they emphasize a close affinity of the Aniu to the Mongoloid stock, especially to the Japanese living in the mainland of Japan. The same results also have been obtained by Kimura (1962) on the basis of finger and palm print patterns and by the present author based on non-metric dental characters (Hanihara, 1968, 1970; Hanihara et al., 1975).

As we have recognized already, the present study reveals the same trend, namely, Ainu are very distant from Aborigines and very close to ordinary Japanese in almost every character studied such as absolute crown size, Mahalanobis' generalized distance, Penrose's shape distance, and Smith's distance. Perhaps the only trait that shows a close affinity between Aborigines and Ainu is the shovelling trait in the maxillary central incisors. However, in general, the present study also supports the recent investigations mentioned above.

7. SUMMARY AND CONCLUSIONS

In this paper several characteristics in the dentition of Australian Aborigines were compared with those of certain other populations from which the data were obtained by the present author. In addition, some other populations which had been studied by previous authors were also included for comparative studies on part of the dental characteristics discussed in this paper. The results are briefly summarized as follows:

1. The deciduous dentition in Aborigines, both males and females, shows the largest mesiodistal crown diameters among the five populations compared—Aborigines, Japanese, Pimas, Caucasians and American Negroes. However, the standard deviations in Aborigines are not significantly different from those of the rest of the populations.

2. The mesiodistal crown diameters of the permanent dentition in Aborigines were compared with those of Japanese, Pimas, Ainu, Caucasians and American Negroes. In general, Aborigines exceed most of the other populations in crown size as in the deciduous dentition. However, Aborigines are rather smaller than Pimas in some teeth. In males, for example, nine teeth out of fourteen represent larger mean values in Pimas than in Aborigines. The most striking difference is recognized in the maxillary canines in which the mean mesiodistal crown diameter in Pimas amount to 106.3% of that of Aborigines. Also in the mandibular canines, Pimas show 104.7% of Aborigines. As a whole, the overall tooth crown size in the deciduous dentition is the largest in Aborigines, but in the permanent dentition, Pimas exceed Aborigines in size of some teeth so that the latter does not necessarily have the largest tooth crown size among the modern human populations.

3. The shovel trait in the maxillary central incisors expressed in terms of depth of the lingual fossa is predominant in Pimas and Japanese, much less in Caucasians and American Negroes, and intermediate in Aborigines and Ainu.

4. Overall between-sex difference in mesiodistal crown diameters in the permanent dentition which is expressed by Mahalanobis' generalized distance shows that Aborigines are similar to Japanese in size component, but to Caucasians and American Negroes in shape component. In addition, Aborigines are quite different from Pimas in either size or shape components. A simple method of comparison reveals that almost the same trends are recognized in between-sex difference of the deciduous dentition.

5. Mesiodistal diameters in the molar crowns were compared between Yuendumu materials and the skulls obtained from Queensland. The average values are, both in males and females, insignificant between the two groups, except for the mandibular second molars in males. As a whole, both groups seem to be almost identical in this character; a minor discrepancy between the two groups appeared to be a random fluctuation.

6. Principal component analysis based on the mesiodistal crown diameters was carried out to reveal the characteristics in each population in terms of principal components. In particular, the present study is concerned with analysis of deciduous and

permanent dentitions in combination. As a result, each population was characterized as follows: Aborigines represent the largest deciduous incisors and molars compared with the other populations, but the permanent incisors and premolars do not necessarily show the largest size among the populations compared; Japanese carry relatively larger deciduous molars; Pimas have the largest permanent incisors, both in absolute size and proportion, relatively small deciduous molars and large premolars; Caucasians generally represent the smallest tooth size, the maxillary lateral incisors being particularly small; and American Negroes carry the smallest deciduous incisors in absolute size and proportion.

7. Affinities between populations were analysed on the basis of Mahalanobis' generalized distance computed from mesiodistal crown diameters of the permanent dentition. The results reveal that Aborigines have a closer affinity to American Negroes and Pimas, relatively far from Japanese and Caucasians, and most far from the northern populations such as Ainu, Aleuts and Norwegian Lapps. In addition, the first canonical variates appear to distinguish the following four clusters in males: Aleut-Ainu cluster, Pima-Javanese-Japanese-Lapp cluster, American Negro-Aborigine cluster, and Swede-Caucasian-Tristanite-American White cluster. In the females, Aborigine-American Negro-Tristanite-Swede-Caucasian-American White cluster, Pima-Japanese-Javanese-Ainu cluster, and Aleut cluster may be distinguished.

8. In order to measure affinities in shape component, Penrose's shape distances were computed from mesiodistal crown diameters in the deciduous and permanent dentitions. Very interestingly, in the shape component, the permanent dentition of Aborigines is close to Caucasians, a little bit far from Japanese and American Negroes, and most far from the northern populations. On the other hand, shape distances in the deciduous dentition show a close affinity between Aborigines and Caucasians as well as Pimas. Although there are some discrepancies in shape distance between the permanent and deciduous dentitions and between males and females, it is noteworthy that Aborigines and Caucasians show in general close affinities in the shape component of the crown measurements.

9. Six non-metric crown characters—shovel trait, cusp 6, cusp 7, deflecting wrinkle, protostylid and Carabelli's cusp—were observed and comparisons between Aborigines and some other populations were carried out on the basis of their frequency distributions. Distance coefficients devised by Smith were used as a tool for such a comparison. In the permanent dentition, Aborigines are close to Mongoloid populations and far from Caucasians, at least the non-metric crown characters are concerned. Trends observed in the deciduous dentition are also quite parallel to those of the permanent dentition. Based on Smith's distances, the following clusters may be distinguished: Aborigine cluster, Japanese-Ainu cluster, Pima-Eskimo cluster, Caucasian cluster and American Negro cluster.

10. From what we mentioned above, it may be concluded that affinities of Aborigines to the populations compared are different from character to character even if the investigations are focused on the dental characters. However, perhaps one fact which may be safely concluded is that Aborigines show a larger extent of archaic dental characters in almost every respect of the present study.

11. Relationship between Aborigines and Ainu was discussed on the basis of

7. Summary and Conclusions

several findings obtained in the present study. The results reveal that Ainu are located very far from Aborigines and very close to ordinary Japanese in almost every character such as absolute crown size and distance coefficients related to size and shape components of crown measurements, and frequency distribution of non-metric crown characters. This strongly supports conclusions obtained by several recent investigations on finger and palm print patterns, skulls and biochemical polymorphisms.

ACKNOWLEDGEMENTS

First of all, the author expresses sincere gratitude to the late Dr Murray J. Barrett who invited him to Adelaide and allowed him to study the excellent dental casts of Aborigines collected by the Department of Dental Science, the University of Adelaide. Without his generosity the data used in this study could not be available. Sincere thanks are due also to Professor A. M. Horsenell and Dr T. Brown of the University of Adelaide for their encouragement during and after the investigation in Adelaide.

The author is also grateful to Dr A. A. Dahlberg of the University of Chicago, Dr T. D. Stewart of U.S. National Museum of Natural History, Dr L. A. Altemus of Howard University in Washington, D. C., and Professor N. W. G. Macintosh of the University of Sydney, for their kind support for studying the dentition of Caucasians, Pima Indians, Eskimos, American Negroes and Queensland Aborigines.

In addition, it should be mentioned here that the investigations in Adelaide were aided by a Leverhulme Visiting Fellowship in Australia to which the author is deeply obliged. Finally the author is indebted to Miss Mariko Izuchi for her assistance in preparing the manuscript of this paper.

REFERENCES

Abbie, A. A. (1951): The Australian Aborigine. *Oceania*, **22**: 91–100.
Abbie, A. A. (1968): The homogeneity of Australian Aborigines. *Archeol. Phys. Anthrop. Oceania*, **3**: 223–231.
Abbie, A. A. (1969): *The Original Australians*. Sydney, A. H. & A. W. Reed.
Barrett, M. J., T. Brown and M. R. Macdonald (1963): Dental observations on Australian aborigines: mesiodistal crown diameters of permanent teeth. *Aust. Dent. J.*, **8**: 150–155.
Barrett, M. J., T. Brown and J. I. Luke (1963): Dental observations on Australian aborigines: mesiodistal crown diameters of deciduous teeth. *Aust. Dent. J.*, **8**: 299–302.
Berry, A. C. and R. J. Berry (1967): Epigenetic variation in the human cranium. *J. Anat.*, **101**: 361–379.
Birdsell, J. B. (1950): Some implications of the genetical concept of race in terms of spatial analysis. *Cold Spring Harbor Symposia on Quantitative Biology*, **15**: 259–311.
Butler, P. M. (1939): Studies of the mammalian dentition. Differentiation of the post-canine dentition. *Proc. Zool. Soc. London*, Ser. B, **109**: 1–36.
Campbell, T. D. (1925): *Dentition and Palate of the Australian Aboriginal*. Adelaide, Univ. of Adelaide.
Carbonell, V. M. (1963): Variations in the frequency of shovel-shaped incisors in different populations. D. R. Brothwell(ed.), *Dental Anthropology*, pp. 211–234, Pergomon Press.
Constandse-Westermann, T. S. (1972): *Coefficients of Biological Distance*. New York, Humanities Press.
Corruccini, R. S. (1973): Size and shape in similarity coefficients based on metric characters. *Am. J. Phys. Anthrop.*, **38**: 743–745.
Dahlberg, A. A. (1945): The changing dentition of man. *J. Am. Dent. Ass.*, **32**: 676–690.
Dahlberg, A. A. (1949): The dentition of the American Indians. W. S. Laughlin (ed.), *Papers on the Physical Anthropology of the American Indians*, pp. 138–176, The Viking Fund, Inc.
Dahlberg, A. A. (1950): The evolutionary significance of the protostylid. *Am. J. Phys. Anthrop.*, **8**: 15–25.
Dahlberg, A. A. and O. Mikkelsen (1949): The shovel-shaped character in the teeth of Pima Indians. *Am. J. Phys. Anthrop.*, **5**: 234–235.
Hanihara, K. (1956): Studies on the deciduous dentition of the Japanese-American hybrids. III. Deciduous lower molars. *J. Anthrop. Soc. Nippon*, **64**: 95–116 (In Japanese with English summary).
Hanihara, K. (1961): Criteria for classification of crown characters in the human deciduous dentition. *J. Anthrop. Soc. Nippon*, **69**: 27–45.
Hanihara, K. (1965): Some crown characters of the deciduous incisors and canines in Japanese-American hybrids. *J. Anthrop. Soc. Nippon*, **72**: 135–145.
Hanihara, K. (1966): Mongoloid dental complex in the deciduous dentition. *J. Anthrop. Soc. Nippon*, **74**: 9–20.
Hanihara, K. (1967): Racial characteristics in the dentition. *J. Dent. Res.*, **46**, Suppl. No. 5, pp. 923–926.
Hanihara, K. (1968): Mongoloid dental complex in the permanent dentition. *Proc. VIIIth Int. Congr. Anthrop. Ethnol. Sci.*, Vol. I, pp. 298–300.

References

Hanihara, K. (1970): Mongoloid dental complex in the deciduous dentition, with special reference to the dentition of the Ainu. *J. Anthrop. Soc. Nippon*, **78**: 3–17.

Hanihara, K. (1974a): Factors controlling crown size of the deciduous dentition. *J. Anthrop. Soc. Nippon*, **82**: 128–134.

Hanihara, K. (1974b): Differences in sexual dimorphism in dental morphology among several human populations. Paper presented to the 4th International Symposium on Dental Morphology.

Hanihara, K. (1976): Distances between Australian Aborigines and certain other populations based on dental measurements. *J. Hum. Evol.* (Under press).

Hanihara, K., T. Kuwashima and N. Sakao (1964): The deflecting wrinkle on the lower molars in recent Japanese. *J. Anthrop. Soc. Nippon*, **72**: 1–8.

Hanihara, K. and T. Minamidate (1965): *Tuberculum accessorium mediale internum* in the human deciduous lower second molars. *J. Anthrop. Soc. Nippon*, **73**: 9–19.

Hanihara, K., T. Tanaka and M. Tamada (1970): Quantitative analysis of the shovel-shaped character in the incisors. *J. Anthrop. Soc. Nippon*, **78**: 90–98.

Hanihara, K., T. Masuda and T. Tanaka (1974): Affinities of dental characteristics in the Okinawa islanders. *J. Anthrop. Soc. Nippon*, **82**: 75–82.

Hanihara, K., T. Masuda, T. Tanaka and M. Tamada (1975): Comparative studies of dentition. Anthropological and Genetic Studies on the Japanese, Part III. Anthropological and Genetic Studies of the Ainu. *JIBP Synthesis*, Vol. 2, pp. 256–262, Tokyo, Univ. of Tokyo Press.

Hayashi, C. (1952): On the prediction of phenomena from qualitative data and the quantification of qualitative data from the mathematico-statistical point of view. *Ann. Inst. Statist. Mathem.*, **3**: 69–98.

Hayashi, C. (1954): Multidimensional quantification with the applications to analysis of social phenomena. *Ann. Inst. Statist. Mathem.*, **5**: 121–143.

Hellman, M. (1928): Racial characters in human dentition. *Proc. Am. Phil. Soc.*, **67**: 157–174.

Hosaka, T. (1936): Statistische Untersuchungen über die Zähne bei Chinesen mit besonderer Berücksichtung der Rassenunterschiede. *J. Orient. Med.*, **24**: 1065–1090, 1230–1251; **25**: 348–368.

Howells, W. W. (1937): Anthropometry of the natives of Arnhem Land and the Australian race problem. *Pap. Peabody Mus.*, **16**: 1–97.

Hrdlička, A. (1920): Shovel-shaped teeth. *Am J. Phys. Anthrop.*, **3**: 429–465.

Jørgensen, K. D. (1956): The deciduous dentition, a descriptive and comparative study. *Acta Odont. Scand.*, **41**, Suppl. 20.

Kimura, K. (1962): The Ainus viewed from their finger and palm prints. *Z. Morph. Anthrop.*, **52**: 176–198.

Kodama, S. (1970): *Ainu, Historical and Anthropological Studies*. Sapporo, Hokkaido Univ. School of Medicine.

von Koenigswald, G. H. R. (1952): *Gigantopithecus blacki* von Koenigswald, a giant fossil hominoid from the Pleistocene of Southern China. *Anthrop. Pap. Am. Mus. Nat. Hist.*, **43**, Pt. 4.

Kuusk, S. (1973): Deciduous tooth crown morphology in a tribe of Australian Aborigines—A study of twelve non-metric traits. Thesis submitted for the degree of Master of Dental Surgery, The University of Adelaide.

Lombardi, A. V. (1975): A factor analysis of morphogenetic fields in the human dentition. *Am. J. Phys. Anthrop.*, **42**: 99–104.

Mijsberg, W. A. (1931): On sexual differences in the teeth of the Javanese. *Koninkl. Akad.*

Wetenschap. Amsterdam, Proc. Sec. Sci., **34**: 1111–1115 (Cited by Moorrees, 1957).
Moorrees, C. F. A. (1957): *The Aleut Dentition, A Correlative Study of Dental Characteristics in an Eskimoid People.* Cambridge, Harvard Univ. Press.
Moorrees, C. F. A., S. O. Thomsen, E. Jensen and P. K. Yen (1957): Mesiodistal crown diameters of the deciduous and permanent teeth in individuals. *J. Dent. Res.*, **36**: 39–47.
Omoto, K. (1972): Polymorphisms and genetic affinities of the Ainu of Hokkaido. *Hum. Biol. Oceania*, **1**: 278–288.
Penrose, L. S. (1954): Distance, size and shape. *Ann. Eug.*, **18**: 337–343.
Rao, C. R. (1952): *Advanced Statistical Methods in Biometric Research.* New York, John Wiley & Sons.
Robinson, J. T. (1956): The dentition of Australopithecinae. *Transvaal Mus. Mem.*, No. 9.
Seipel, C. M. (1946): Variation of tooth position. *Svensk Tandläkare-Tidskr.*, Suppl. to Vol. 39 (Cited by Moorrees, 1957).
Selenka, E. (1898): Rassen, Schädel und Bezahnung des Orangutan. Menschenaffen (Anthropomorphae), Pt. 1: 1–91, Wiesbaden (Cited by Weidenreich, 1945).
Selmer-Olsen, R. (1949): An odontometrical study on the Norwegian Lapps. *Skrifter utgitt av det Norske Videnskaps—Akademi Oslo*, I. Mat.-Naturv. Klasse No. 3 (Cited by Moorrees, 1957).
Sokal, R. R. and P. H. A. Sneath (1963): *Principles of Numerical Taxonomy.* San Francisco, Freeman.
Suzuki, M. and T. Sakai (1954): On the "protostylid" of the Japanese. *J. Anthrop. Soc. Nippon*, **63**: 81–84 (In Japanese with English summary).
Suzuki, M. and T. Sakai (1956a): On the "Dryopithecus pattern" in recent Japanese. *J. Anthrop. Soc. Nippon*, **64**: 87–94 (In Japanese with English summary).
Suzuki, M. and T. Sakai (1956b): On the "tuberculum accessorium mediale internum" in recent Japanese. *J. Anthrop. Soc. Nippon*, **64**: 135–139 (In Japanese with English summary).
Suzuki, M. and T. Sakai (1956c): On the "deflecting wrinkle" in recent Japanese. *J. Anthrop. Soc. Nippon*, **65**: 49–53 (In Japanese with English summary).
de Terra, M. (1905): Beiträge zu einer Odontographie der Menschenrassen. Inaug. Diss. Phil., Zurich (Cited by Weidenreich, 1945).
Thomsen, S. (1955): Dental morphology and occlusion in the people of Tristan da Cunha, 1937–1938, No. 25, Oslo (Cited by Moorrees, 1957).
Tindale, N. B. and J. B. Birdsell (1941): Results of the Harvard-Adelaide Universities anthropological expedition, 1938–1939. Tasmanoid tribes in North Queensland. *Rec. South Aust. Mus.*, **7**: 1–9 (Cited by Yamaguchi, 1967).
Tratman, E. K. (1950): A comparison of the teeth of people, Indo-European racial stock with the Mongoloid racial stock. *Dent. Rec.*, **70**: 31–53, 63–88.
Weidenreich, F. (1937): The dentition of *Sinanthropus pekinensis:* A comparative odontography of the hominids. *Palaeont. Sinica*, n.s.D, No. 1.
Weidenreich, F. (1945): Giant early man from Java and South China. *Anthrop. Pap. Am. Mus. Nat. Hist.*, **40**, Pt. 1.
Yamaguchi, B. (1967): *A Comparative Osteological Study of the Ainu and Australian Aborigines.* Canberra, Australian Institute of Aboriginal Studies.